GLOBETROTTER™

P9-ASJ-024

Travel Guide

SOUTH
AFRICA

PETER JOYCE

NEW
HOLLAND

NEW
HOLLAND

This edition first published in 2001
by New Holland Publishers (UK) Ltd
London • Cape Town • Sydney • Auckland
First published in 1994
10 9 8 7 6 5 4 3 2

Garfield House, 86 Edgware Road
London W2 2EA
United Kingdom

80 McKenzie Street
Cape Town, 8001
South Africa

14 Aquatic Drive
Frenchs Forest, NSW 2086
Australia

218 Lake Road
Northcote, Auckland
New Zealand

Commissioning Editor: Tim Jollands
Manager Globetrotter Maps: John Loubser
Managing Editor: Thea Grobbelaar
Editors: Tarryn Berry, Marielle Renssen, Brenda
Brickman, Sean Fraser
Designers: Lellyn Creamer, Lyndall Hamilton
Cartographer: Genené Hart

Reproduction by Hirt & Carter (Pty) Ltd, Cape Town
Printed and bound in Hong Kong by Sing Cheong
Printing Co. Ltd.

Acknowledgements:
The publishers wish to thank the following for their
co-operation with the photographers involved in this
project: Blydepoort Resort, the KwaZulu Department
of Nature Conservation, the Oceanarium in Port
Elizabeth, the Nature Conservation Service of
KwaZulu-Natal, National Parks of South Africa and
Sun International.

Photographic credits:
Shaen Adey, pages 7, 25, 36, 107 (top), 73, 78, 82, 88;
Gerald Cubitt, pages 21, 22, 23, 37; **Roger de la
Harpe**, pages 26 (top right), 77, 98; **Nigel Dennis**,
pages 11, 58; **Walter Knirr**, pages 15, 26 (bottom
right), 30, 34, 38, 39, 41, 43, 46, 49, 50, 51, 62, 65, 66,
67, 68, 69, 74, 75, 102, 108, 109, 110, 111, 112, 115, 116
(top); **John McKinnell**, page 87; **Nicola Newman**,
page 27; **Marek Patzer**, page 26 (bottom left); **Struik
Image Library Struik [SIL]**, page 28; **SIL/Shaen
Adey**, pages 35, 75, 105 113; **SIL/Roger de la Harpe**,
pages 71, 72, 79; **SIL/Nigel Dennis**, pages 54, 56, 59
(top and bottom); **SIL/Gerhard Dreyer**, pages 4, 92,
95, 97, 119; **SIL/Walter Knirr**, cover, title page,
pages 19, 42, 52, 55; **SIL/Jackie Murray**, page 14;
SIL/Peter Pickford, pages 6, 53, 57, 116 (bottom),
118; **SIL/Erhardt Thiel**, pages 26 (top left), 29, 106,
107 (bottom), 114; **SIL/Hein von Hörsten**, pages 8,
10; **SIL/Lanz von Hörsten**, page 117; **SIL/Keith
Young**, page 94; **The Argus Newspaper**, page 17;
Colin Urquhart, pages 86, 99; **Mark van Aardt**,
pages 16, 89, 96 ; **Keith Young**, page 85.
[SIL: Struik Image Library]

Cover: *A lone windmill, Free State.*
Title page: *Table Mountain, Western Cape.*

CONTENTS

1
Introducing
South Africa

South Africa covers an area of well over a million square kilometres (386,000 square miles) of the southern subcontinent. To the east, north and west it is bounded by the republics of Namibia, Botswana, Zimbabwe and Mozambique, and enclosed within its borders are the kingdoms of Lesotho and Swaziland.

A country rich in diversity, South Africa's contrasts are strikingly apparent in the bewildering mix of culture and language. Variety is there, too, in the character of the cities and the nature of the land. Eastwards from the modern metropolis of Johannesburg lies the rugged Escarpment which falls rapidly away to the humid, sub-tropical Lowveld with its world-famous Kruger National Park. Southwards lies KwaZulu-Natal, with its own compliment of bushveld, wetland and marine reserves. Durban, a harbour city fringed by golden beaches, is the third largest conurbation in the country. In contrast to the string of coastal towns and resorts south of Durban, is the spectacular and unspoilt Wild Coast, of the Eastern Cape Province. Along South Africa's southern shores, lies the Garden Route, a place of gentle beauty, comprising seaside towns, forests and lakes, against the backdrop of the Outeniqua mountains. The westward journey through the rich Western Cape farmlands and along South Africa's southern seaboard culminates in the Cape Peninsula and the city of Cape Town, at the foot of Table Mountain, and its surrounds – the Winelands – a magical setting of craggy peaks and secluded valleys with their vineyards, orchards and historic homesteads.

TOP ATTRACTIONS

*** Kruger National Park: One of the world's best known wildlife conservation areas.
*** Cape Town: South Africa's historical 'Mother City' with Table Mountain, Cape Point and the Winelands.
** Casino/leisure complexes: some 40 grand venues around the country.
** The Garden Route: South Africa's Eden stretches 200km (125 miles) along the Western Cape's south coast.
** Northern KwaZulu-Natal: Maputaland game reserves and St Lucia wetlands.
** The Drakensberg: Holiday resorts among South Africa's highest peaks.

Opposite: *Wilderness, on the 'Garden Route'.*

FACTS AND FIGURES

• **Highest mountains** are the Drakensberg, peaking at Champagne Castle (3376m;11,077ft), which is just one of the range's many awesome buttresses.
• **Longest river** is the Gariep (Orange), which flows for some 2250km (1400 miles) from east to west.
• **Largest waterfall** (and one of the world's six largest) is the Augrabies on the Gariep River; in a series of 19 cataracts tumbling 146m (479ft).
• **Deepest gorge** is the Blyde River Canyon in Mpumalanga – up to 800m (2625ft) deep and 1.5km (1 mile) wide in places.

Below: *The lower reaches of the Gariep, South Africa's largest river.*
Opposite: *Wolfberg Arch is one of the Cederberg's many dramatic wind-sculpted rock formations.*

THE LAND

In broad geophysical terms, South Africa can be divided into just two regions. The greater is the semicircular interior plateau, varying in altitude from the central region of the Great Karoo (a flat, semi-desert area that covers around 400,000km² or 154,440 sq miles), to the towering Drakensberg in the east (the loftiest segment of a necklace of mountains known as the Great Escarpment). The second region is a narrow coastal belt fringing the plateau on three sides.

Mountains and Rivers

The grandest of the country's heights are those of the **Drakensberg**, the spectacular eastern part of the Great Escarpment, whose gigantic basalt face falls almost sheer for a full 2000m (6565 feet) to the green midlands of KwaZulu-Natal. So formidable is the rampart that the main 250-km (155 miles) stretch can only be negotiated by one route – the Sani Pass.

Formed by a quite different geological process are what are known as the Cape Fold mountains, a series that runs parallel to the southern coast. Here, rising majestically over wide valleys, are the **Swartberg** and **Tsitsikamma**, the **Outeniqua** and the **Langeberg**.

Inland, beyond the lovely winelands of the west, are the **Hottentots-Holland**, the **Drakenstein**, and the rugged **Cederberg** – place of strangely eroded rocks, of caves, deep ravines and streams, and home to the rare Clanwilliam cedar tree and the pure-white snow protea (*Protea cryophila*).

And then, of course, there is world-renowned **Table Mountain** and its attendant heights, great sandstone buttresses that run south from the city of Cape Town towards Cape Point.

A number of the country's rivers rise in the KwaZulu-Natal's Drakensberg, eight alone on the aptly named **Mont-aux-Sources** (mountain of springs) massif.

Many of these, including the Tugela, cut their way down the eastern slopes, and over the eastern coastal plain to discharge into the Indian Ocean.

South Africa's largest watercourse, the **Gariep (Orange) River**, on the other hand, flows west across the sub-continent plunging magnificently through the Augrabies gorge, close to the Namibian border, before embarking on its last, desolate stretch to the Atlantic Ocean. Though much of its course crosses arid, treeless terrain, its waters are increasingly being used to irrigate flanking farmlands.

Among the Gariep's bigger tributaries is the **Vaal**, longer but less voluminous than the Gariep. The Western Cape's **Olifants** and beautiful **Berg**, the **Breede,** the **Sundays** and **Great Fish** in the Eastern Cape, and the **Limpopo**, which marks the country's border with Zimbabwe, are other significant rivers.

South Africa's rivers, though, do not amount to very much in world terms. Put together their total run-off is barely equal to that of the Rhine at Rotterdam, and to just half that of the mighty Zambezi 1000 kilometres (620 miles) to the north.

Seas and Shores

The country's coastline presents a striking study in contrasts. The western seaboard's rocky, windblown shorelines backed by raised beaches stretching inland for up to 50km (31 miles), and washed by the cold **Benguela Current**, does have its attractions: a wealth of seabirds (gannets, cormorants and terns roost and nest on the offshore islands), charming fishing villages, and, for a few brief springtime weeks, a countryside magically transformed by great carpets of wildflowers.

The south and east coasts, are washed by the warmer waters of the **Agulhas Current**, and in tourist terms are more popular. In the south, the 220-km (135 miles) Garden Route, stretching roughly from Heidelberg to the Storms River, is very beautiful; its forested coastal terrace

---

RIVER RAFTING: ALL THE RAGE

A popular way to enjoy the beauty and excitement of South Africa's rivers is to join a group of river rafters or canoeists. No experience is necessary as experts are at hand to show you the ropes and ensure your safety and comfort. It is best to join a party organized by one of the five or six reputable operators. Trips lasting between one and four days negotiate stretches of the following major watercourses:

• **Gariep River**, which runs through the Northern Cape and along the southern border of Namibia.

• **Breede River** near Swellendam in the Western Cape (one operator includes a wine-tasting session on the itinerary!).

• **Tugela River**, which flows over some challenging rapids in central KwaZulu-Natal.

• **Sabie River** in lovely Mpumalanga (rafting on this watercourse is subject to seasonal rains).

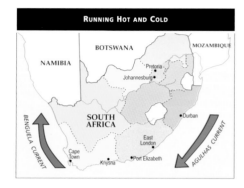

RUNNING HOT AND COLD

is overlooked by not-too-distant
Outeniqua mountains. Equally
enticing to holiday-makers are the
wide expanses of golden sand and
the sun-drenched resorts to either
side of Durban on the east coast.

Climate

Weather patterns, dictated by
ocean currents, altitude, prevail-
ing wind and the ever-changing
nature of the land, vary dramat-
ically from place to place.

When it comes to rainfall, though, there are three
broad (but distinct) regions. The southwestern tip of
South Africa, centring on the lovely city of **Cape Town**,
has a **winter rainfall** (May to August).

The **southern** and **eastern coastal belts** of South Africa
enjoy **perennial showers** which are heavy – almost

*Below: East London, a
major river-port in the
Eastern Cape, is known
for it's beaches – two
magnificent stretches of
sand that are popular
among fishermen, as well
as sun-worshippers.*

tropical – in KwaZulu-Natal, especially in summer. Rains
over the rest of the country – on the great **central plateau**
and in the **Lowveld** to the east – come irregularly and
suddenly, with heavy **summer thunderstorms**.

Which is not to say that the land as a whole is well
watered. On the contrary, South Africa is one of the world's
drier countries: mean annual rainfall is only 464mm (18
in), little more than half the global average.

Only a third of the country gets
enough rain for non-irrigated
farming; just a quarter has perennial rivers, and even these are
subject to seasonal flow.

Plant Life

Vegetation as everywhere, is influenced by the climate, ranging from
the hardy succulents, aloes and
spring-flowering desert annuals of
the parched western seaboard and
the vast west-central wastelands

to the mountain pines and dense lowland bushveld of the moist northeast. Much of the inland plateau – especially the central and northern regions – consists of endless rolling grasslands which, because of the winter droughts and frosts, has few trees. Indeed, only a tiny part of the country is covered by natural forests,

COMPARATIVE CLIMATE CHART	JOHANNESBURG				DURBAN				CAPE TOWN			
	SUM	AUT	WIN	SPR	SUM	AUT	WIN	SPR	SUM	AUT	WIN	SPR
	JAN	APR	JULY	OCT	JAN	APR	JULY	OCT	JAN	APR	JULY	OCT
MIN TEMP. °C	15	11	5	12	21	17	10	17	15	10	8	13
MAX TEMP. °C	25	21	16	24	28	26	23	24	26	20	18	23
MIN TEMP. °F	59	52	41	54	70	63	50	63	59	50	46	55
MAX TEMP. °F	77	70	61	75	82	79	73	75	79	68	64	73
HOURS OF SUN	8	8	9	9	6	7	7	5	11	7	7	10
RAINFALL mm	131	55	6	72	135	87	44	89	17	77	70	20
RAINFALL in	5	2	0.5	3	5	3	2	4	1	3	3	1

the largest a magical strip of tall ironwoods, yellowwoods and stinkwoods in the Knysna-Tsitsikamma area.

Further to the north, along KwaZulu-Natal's Indian Ocean shoreline, there are patches of evergreen subtropical trees, including palms and, in the swampier areas, mangroves.

Wild Kingdom

South Africa's prime tourist attraction is without doubt its magnificent wildlife heritage, seen at its most spectacular in the big-game areas of Mpumalanga (formerly known as the Eastern Transvaal) and KwaZulu-Natal – areas well frequented by international visitors. In terms of overall species diversity, South Africa ranks third in the world, bested only by Indonesia and the Amazonian forests.

There are more then 20 national parks (a few are very new and still under development) and about 300 smaller regional and local reserves in South Africa, some created primarily to protect wild animals, others the unique plant life or distinctive scenic character of a region. The largest and best known of these is the **Kruger National Park**, where the great diversity of wildlife includes the 'big five' – lion, leopard, rhino, elephant and buffalo – and some 500 different species of birds. In addition to the many tourist camps in the Park, there is a choice of luxurious lodges situated in the private game reserves along its western boundary. Impressive, too, are the reserves of **Northern KwaZulu-Natal**, where varied vegetation types provide ideal habitats for a similarly impressive array of animals and birds, including a wide range of waterbirds. Quite different in character but equally attractive is the **Kgalagadi Transfrontier Park**, a vast wilderness of Kalahari dunes, sandy plains, thornbush and scanty grassland which is home to cheetah, lion, wild dog and herds of antelope. It's two segments – one in northern South Africa, the other in southern Botswana – were recently combined to create Africa's first cross-border or 'peace' park (see below).

SUNNY SOUTH AFRICA

South Africa has one of the world's most equitable climates; the average number of **cloudless hours** a day varies from **8** to **10** compared with New York's 7, Rome's 6 and London's modest 4.

Rainfall is low over most of the country, and some areas – particularly the dust-dry western region – record a bare 10 or so overcast days a year.

Below Right: *Elephants in the Addo Elephant National Park, refuge for the remnants of the once-great Cape herds.*

Conserving South Africa's Natural Heritage

South Africa's wild regions, like those elsewhere in Africa, are under threat – from urban sprawl, alienplant species, industry and mining, livestock, farmlands, and, particularly, the pressure on natural resources by impoverished rural communities.

But there is hope. Society's priorities are changing, and the voice of the conservationist is being heard much more clearly today. Moreover, decision-makers are starting to recognize that ecotourism can generate vast amounts of money and huge job opportunities. There is now a general conviction that the wellbeing of the wildlife and the interests of tourism need not conflict with the needs of rural people. There are exciting plans to extend the areas of conservation, even beyond the political borders. Until now, human encroachment has confined the animals within relatively small spaces; the expanded wildernesses will re-open the ancient migratory routes, returning at least some of the game-rich land to its original, pristine condition. The Kgalagadi, as mentioned, is the first such enterprise. Similar cross-border sanc-tuaries are being developed or planned for the northern KwaZulu-Natal region, the Limpopo Valley and the Lowveld (which will bring together South Africa's Kruger National Park, Zimbabwe's Gonarezhou and part of southern Mozambique.

SPOT THE BIG FIVE

Top of the game-viewing list are the Big Five, all of which can be spotted in the Kruger National Park.
• The **lion**, largest of Africa's carnivores, is most active at night, but it can be seen feeding on the remains of a kill in daylight. Lion sleep some 20 hours a day.
• The **leopard**, a shy, solitary creature, is a nocturnal hunter. Its dappled coat provides excellent camouflage.
• Some 7500 or more **elephant** roam in the Kruger, home of South Africa's great tuskers.
• The **white rhino**, despite its name, is grey in colour and is identified by its square-lipped mouth. The smaller **black rhino** is also grey in colour (not black), and is recognized by its 'hooked' upper lip.
• The **buffalo**, usually a placid animal, can be extremely dangerous when threatened or provoked.

HISTORY IN BRIEF

Millennia ago, long before the arrival of the white man in southern Africa, bands of nomadic Bushman (or San) hunter-gatherers roamed the great spaces in search of sustenance. About 2000 years ago some of the groups, having acquired sheep from the Sudanic peoples of the north, were introduced for the first time to the concept of property ownership and territory. The wealthier and more powerful San, known as Khoikhoi (Hottentots) concentrated in loose federations. They eventually divided, some migrating to the Cape Peninsula. These were the first southern Africans to come into contact with the European seafarers of the 16th century. Meanwhile, peoples of quite different cultures – Bantu-speakers who used iron and kept cattle – had occupied parts of what is now Zimbabwe in the far north, to be followed, around AD 1100 by a second and stronger migratory wave that washed south through the great interior and down the east coast. By the 17th century its vanguard, the Xhosa, were advancing along the southern seaboard on a direct collision course with the European colonists.

The Clash of Cultures

Although the Portuguese navigators (notably Dias and Da Gama) pioneered the sea route to India in the years between 1488 and 1497, it was the Dutch who first

Above: *The lovely silver tree, largest of the extensive protea family.*

CAPE FLORAL KINGDOM

- The **Cape Floral Kingdom** is the smallest, but richest, of the world's six floral kingdoms.
- The vegetation type is known collectively as **fynbos** ('fine bush') and includes the lovely ericas (800 species) and proteas (the king protea is South Africa's national flower).
- More plant species occur on **Table Mountain** than are found in the entire British Isles.
- Many of the species are unique to the area.
- Make a point of visiting **Kirstenbosch National Botanical Gardens**, which has a spectacular year-round display of indigenous flowering plants, that attract many different bird species, in particular, the pretty sunbirds.

EARLY MAN

Southern and East Africa are widely regarded as the **Cradle of Mankind**, where humans' first ancestors appeared. Renowned palaeontologist **Raymond Dart** uncovered the first important hominid remains – a million-year-old infant skull – at **Taung**, in the northern Cape in 1924, naming the species *Australopithecus africanus*. Finds by **Robert Broom** in the **Sterkfontein Caves** between 1936 and 1947, confirmed the link between ape-like creatures and early man. Sterkfontein and its neighbours are now a World Heritage Site.

established a permanent presence on the southern tip of Africa. In April 1652, Jan van Riebeeck and his small party arrived on the shores of the bay beneath Table Mountain to create a victualling station for the Dutch East India Company's passing fleets. Eventually, a shortage of food prompted Van Riebeeck to release a number of Company officials from their employment contracts to set themselves up as farmers. He also imported slaves from other parts of Africa and from the Far East.

Both moves were significant. Having developed into a colony capable of growth, the Cape outpost expanded steadily over the following decades as 'trekboers' and farmers took their sheep and cattle and moved into the hinterland, pushing the Cape's boundaries ever outward. In the east they came up against the Xhosa, and competition for grazing land inevitably led to confrontation. In 1779 the first of nine bloody 'frontier wars' erupted.

Colonial Expansion

By the end of the century the power of the Netherlands was in decline, and in 1795 the British took over at the Cape. They withdrew for a brief period eight years later, returning in 1806 to rule the colony for the rest of the 19th century, during which white settlement expanded to cover the entire South African region. The story unfolded in three main areas of conflict.

In 1820 the colonial government, convinced that only large-scale immigration would bring stability to the **eastern Cape** region, brought in some 4000 British settlers. For a time it seemed that borders could be agreed, and that the Xhosa would be left in peace, but eventually the settlers resumed their eastward push, and the black clans were progressively subdued.

Meanwhile the far eastern seaboard was also being colonized: British hunters and traders began to settle in **Port Natal** (now Durban) during the 1820s. Their arrival coincided with the *Mfecane* (*Difaqane* in Sotho), a catastrophic series of forced marches triggered by the meteoric rise to power of the Zulu king **Shaka**: his newly fashioned army set out on a bloody war of conquest, igniting a chain reaction of violence and counterviolence that engulfed the entire east coast and much of the interior. During the 1830s, other whites rolled in from the west in their ox-wagons, **Boer (Afrikaner) trekkers** who came into conflict with Shaka's successor, Dingane, whom they finally defeated at Blood River in 1838. But it was the British who eventually prevailed – over both trekker and Zulu. The former were eased out of the fledgling colony of Natal in 1843; the latter, after a stunning victory at **Isandhlwana**, were crushed at **Ulundi** in 1879.

By the 1830s many Dutch-speaking Cape settlers, disenchanted with the British authorities at the Cape and incensed by the formal abolition of slavery in 1834 (which deprived the farmers of cheap labour), began to head into the interior in a mass migration known as the **Great Trek**.

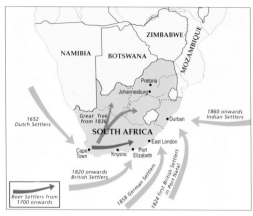

Colonial Migration

The exodus gathered momentum over the next few turbulent years, and eventually white people controlled much of the territory north of the Gariep River. In the early 1850s their settlements were entrenched and strong enough to warrant the creation of two independent Boer republics: the **Orange Free State** and the **Transvaal**.

War and Union

The discovery of the fabulous **Kimberley** diamond fields at the end of the 1860s, and of the Witwatersrand's golden reef 25 years later, however, destroyed any chance of lasting peace between Boer and Briton. The northern region had become a prize worth competing for. Britain and the Transvaal fought it out on the slopes of **Majuba Hill** in Natal in 1881 (the Boers won) in a battle that left the former humiliated and the latter, in the person of Paul Kruger, deeply suspicious of British imperial intentions. In the event, Kruger's suspicions were to be vindicated – most notably by the abortive Jameson Raid of 1896/7, and in 1899 the two countries went to war again.

The Anglo-Boer conflict lasted nearly three years, reduced much of the northern countryside to a barren wilderness and left a legacy of bitterness. The British, however, were determined on reconciliation. Their peace terms, set out in the **Treaty of Vereeniging** (1902), were

---

SHAKA: WARRIOR SUPREME

When Shaka succeeded to the Zulu chieftainship in 1816, the Zulu numbered just 1500 people – but within a few years he controlled the entire eastern (KwaZulu-Natal) seaboard. The keys to this phenomenal expansion were the new weapons and fighting techniques he introduced to his army, among them:

• The **assegai**, a short, stabbing weapon introduced to replace the spears which had been hurled from ineffectual distances.
• Shaka split the young men of the various clans into **Zulu regiments** according to age, ensuring loyalty to the throne rather than to the headman.
• The famed Zulu battle formation (known as the **impi**), comprising the central 'chest' for frontal attack and the two 'horns' for encirclement.

THE BATTLEFIELDS

Relics of the many great
battles fought in the 19th
century in KwaZulu-Natal
can be seen along the
Battlefields Route at:
• **Blood River** (1838):
Voortrekkers defeat the
Zulus; a 'laager' of 63 full-
size bronze ox-wagons
marks the battlefield.
• **Isandhlwana** (1879): Zulus
annihilate a British army.
• **Rorkes Drift** (1879): a
small British force holds out
against massive Zulu attack;
11 Victoria Crosses are sub-
sequently awarded.
• **Majuba Hill** (1881): Boers
defeat a British army to win
the Transvaal war.
• **Spioenkop** (1900): Boers
capture the hill after one of
the bloodiest of Anglo-Boer
War battles.

generous to the defeated Afrikaners, and on 31 May 1910
the former Boer republics (Transvaal and Orange Free
State) and the two British colonies (Cape and Natal) were
united to become provinces of the new **Union of South
Africa**. The country's first prime minister was Louis
Botha, his deputy Jan Smuts, both Afrikaners of the
'enlightened' (pro-British) kind. The black people had
not been consulted in the creation of the unified state,
and had no democratic rights within the new order.

Afrikanerdom Takes Over

The years between Union in 1910 and the crucial 1948
general election saw South Africa's transformation into a
powerful, modern, industrial nation. They were years of
profound social change – and of a growing racial divide.

The legal separation of black and white – later known
as **apartheid** – had always, even in the old 'liberal' Cape
colony, been a part of the South African fabric. The
Transvaal republic, for its part, had bluntly stated it
would 'permit no equality between coloured people and
the white inhabitants, either in Church or State'. After
Union, the racial gap widened.

World War I stimulated industry and the growth of
urban areas. At the same time tens of thousands of people
were being forced off the land – initially by cattle disease
and the Anglo-Boer conflict, later by mechanization,
always by drought. The blacks gathered around the cities

Below: *'Oom' Paul Kruger,
the father of Afrikanerdom,
gazes across Pretoria's
Church Square. Below
him stands the figure
of a Boer soldier.*

in huge, strictly controlled
locations, the 'poor whites'
(mainly Afrikaners who
could not compete with
cheap African labour) on
the fringes. Conflict was
inevitable. The economic
depression heightened
insecurity among the
white wage-earners, and
strikes and unrest became
a regular feature of the
between-wars years.

In this tense climate, successive Union governments pushed through new racial measures ranging from job reservation and urban segregation to the formal allocation of land to confine the rural Africans. The moves, though, failed to satisfy the hardliners, a section of whom formed the extremist **Reunited National Party** in 1934 under the leadership of D.F. Malan, which steadily gained support among whites during the next decade. Jan Smuts, who led the country through the difficult years of World War II, badly underestimated this radical movement, and in 1948 Malan was elected to office to form South Africa's first all-Afrikaner government.

Above: *Pretoria's Union Buildings, the 1910 monument to Boer–Briton reconciliation.*

Below: *The statue of Paul Kruger in Pretoria.*

The Apartheid Years

Although the nationalists of the 1950s and 1960s did not invent apartheid, they did tie together the existing threads of race prejudice to create one of the most all-embracing bodies of restrictive law ever devised. The **Group Areas Act** (1950) segregated even further the country's cities and towns. Other laws involved racially based identity documents (the so-called **Pass Laws**), the classification of people according to colour, segregation of amenities ('whites-only' signs went up throughout the country) and the prohibition of mixed marriages and sex across the colour line. It was Hendrik Verwoerd, as Minister of Native Affairs (1950–58) and later as prime minister, who contrived much of this, as

well as the massively destructive Bantu Education Act condemning blacks to inferior schooling. He also laid the foundations of the homelands system – the **'Grand Apartheid'** design that carried segregation to its insane conclusion. Verwoerd died in 1966, victim of a a knife-wielding assassin. Other major events during his ruthless premiership were the Sharpeville shootings (1960); the subsequent banning of the **African National Congress (ANC)** and other opposition groups; South Africa's expulsion from the Commonwealth and its transitions from dominion to republic (1961).

FIRST STEPS TO FREEDOM

Among the high points of the liberation struggle in the early apartheid years were the award of the **Nobel Peace Prize** to **Albert Luthuli**, who became president of the African National Congress (ANC) in 1952, and the signing of the **Freedom Charter** in 1955. The Charter, a crucial document that provided the framework of future protest, stated that South Africa belonged to all its people, black, brown and white, and went on to advocate:

• A nonracial democracy
• Equal rights and protection before the law
• Equality in job and educational opportunities
• The redistribution of the land as well as the nationalization of banks, mines and heavy industries.

The Liberation Movement

The black opposition generally and the ANC in particular had its roots in the disillusionment that set in after the Anglo-Boer War, a sense of betrayal reinforced by the exclusion of the black majority from the process leading up to Union in 1910. Nevertheless the ANC, formed as the **South African Native National Congress** (1912–1925), remained committed to peaceful solutions for the next half century. It retained its non-racial, liberal stance even during the bitterly waged 'defiance campaign' of the early 1950s. This moderation, which had singly failed to advance the cause, prompted a breakaway by radical elements who, in 1959, formed the **Pan-Africanist Congress (PAC)**. A year later, following the massacre at Sharpeville, both bodies were banned in terms of the **Unlawful Organisations Act** and went underground.

The ANC launched its armed wing, **Umkhonto we Sizwe** (Spear of the Nation), and embarked on a wide-ranging programme of sabotage that led, in 1963, to the arrest of **Nelson Mandela** and other prominent Congress figures. In the following year, at the celebrated 'Rivonia Trial', they were sentenced to life imprisonment and consigned to **Robben Island**, near Cape Town.

Protest and Reform

Sharpeville, where 69 demonstrators had been gunned down by police, was a crucial turning point in the country's affairs. Before the shootings South Africa, for all the criticism levelled at it, was an accepted member of the community of nations; after March 1960 it faced isolation abroad and mounting race conflict at home.

Verwoerd's successors, B.J. Vorster (1966-78) and P.W. Botha (1978-1990) tried hard to stem the tide – the former through a policy of 'detente' with independent black states, the latter through, among other things, a programme of domestic reform. Botha's new constitution gave the Indian and Coloured communities a political voice, albeit a limited one, but once again Africans were excluded from the central process (they were deemed to be citizens of one or other of the artificially created 'homelands') and the initiative was doomed from the start.

The seeds of failure, in fact, had been sown much earlier – in June 1976, when the ideas of a talented activist named **Steve Biko** (he later died in police custody) had taken root on university campuses and in the townships. Biko, founder of the radical 'black consciousness' movement, urged Africans to take pride in their self-sufficiency, in their colour and culture, and insisted that white people would be irrelevant in a 'post-Revolutionary South Africa'. Tensions came to a head when the use of Afrikaans as a teaching medium was enforced in black schools. Powerful contributing factors, of course, were the denial of citizenship, general discrimination and lack of civic facilities. On 16 June 1976 when some 10, 000 students staged a protest march

Opposite: *Robben Island, onetime 'political' prison, counted Nelson Mandela as its most illustrious inmate. The island is now a World Heritage Site.*
Below: *De Klerk and Mandela, architects of the New South Africa.*

HISTORICAL CALENDAR

AD 200 First Bantu-speaking peoples enter South Africa; present basic pattern of black settlement established by the year 1500.

1497 Da Gama rounds Cape, charts sea route to India.

1652 Dutch settlers land at Cape, begin to colonize the interior; slaves imported.

1779 First of nine settler-Xhosa 'frontier wars' breaks out in Eastern Cape.

1806 British occupy Cape to govern for remainder of the century.

1824 White traders establish a community at Port Natal (now Durban).

1834 Slavery abolished.

1836-38 Great Trek begins as Boer (Afrikaner) families move into the interior.

1852-54 Transvaal and Orange Free State become independent Boer republics.

1869-70 Kimberley diamond fields discovered.

1886 Witwatersrand gold fields discovered; Johannesburg founded.

1899-1902 Anglo-Boer War; Boer guerillas resist fiercely but are eventually defeated.

1910 Unification of South Africa (Union).

1912 SANNC (later called the ANC) is founded.

1948 Afrikaner nationalists win election; apartheid is launched.

1960–61 Sharpeville massacre; South Africa leaves Commonwealth to become republic; liberation organizations banned.

1964 Nelson Mandela and others imprisoned 'for life'.

1976 Soweto students revolt; disturbances spread.

1989 F.W. de Klerk replaces P.W. Botha as president.

1990 Nelson Mandela is released from prison.

1994 Democratic elections; Mandela inaugurated as president on 10 May.

1999 Thabo Mbeki succeeds Mandela as president.

LEADING LIGHTS

In 1993 two South African leaders shared the Nobel Peace Prize for their part in launching the country on the path to democracy:

Nelson Rolihlahla Mandela, leader of the ANC: born 1918; qualified as lawyer 1942; banned under Suppression of Communism Act, 1952; helped found ANC military wing 1961; arrested for conspiring to promote sabotage and insurrection 1963; imprisoned 1964; released 1990.

Frederick Willem de Klerk, state president: born 1936; active in student politics; qualified as lawyer; elected leader of Transvaal National Party and known as hardline conservative until 1989 when he introduced far-reaching political reforms.

---

through the streets of Soweto and then battled it out with the security forces. Lives were lost, buildings and vehicles destroyed, and the violence spread to other parts of the country, continuing for another eight months. These riots, and the troubled years that followed, established a pattern – of unrest designed to 'make the country ungovernable', of tough police reaction, of a regime increasingly under siege. By the late 1980s the townships were in a state of anarchy, and even conservative whites were convinced that they could no longer hold onto power.

The New Era

In 1989 the ailing P.W. Botha was ousted in favour of **F.W. de Klerk**, a politician not noted for his liberal views but a pragmatist nevertheless. The changes that followed were rapid, fundamental, and dramatic. On 2 February 1990, at the opening session of parliament, De Klerk announced the unbanning of the ANC, the South African Communist Party, the PAC and other organizations. Two weeks later **Nelson Mandela**, behind bars for the past 27 years, walked to freedom. The decades of white political supremacy had finally come to an end; the new South Africa was about to be born.

GOVERNMENT AND ECONOMY

A new system of government; the future direction of the economy; redistribution of wealth; in fact, the entire restructuring of society – these were the issues fundamental to the negotiation process that began in 1991. Discussions over the next three years were complex and plagued by setbacks, and by a political arena that was fraught with violence. By the beginning of 1994,

Above: A symbolic composite figure of the bull and bear graces the interior of the now largely electronic Johannesburg Securities Exchange.

however, the protagonists – the leaders of more than 20 political parties meeting at the World Trade Centre near Johannesburg – had reached agreement, and the route to a new democratic dispensation had been successfully charted.

Key elements of the concord were an **interim constitution**, which made provision for a **government of national unity**, a **National Assembly** of 400 members elected by universal suffrage, and for a federal framework encompassing nine **provincial assemblies**. During its five-year life the National Assembly, working within a predetermined formula, would produce a **final constitution** and a comprehensive **Bill of Rights**.

One-person, one-vote elections, held at the end of April 1994, gave the African National Congress a 62 per cent majority in the National Assembly, clear majorities in six of the provincial legislatures and a slender majority in the seventh. Chief Mangosuthu Buthelezi's **Inkatha Freedom Party** won the KwaZulu-Natal province, F.W. de Klerk's Nationalists the Western Cape.

On 10 May, in the amphitheatre of Pretoria's historic Union Buildings, and to an audience of foreign dignitaries numbering more than have been seen together at any

SOUTH AFRICA'S FOREIGN EARNINGS

- Precious metals (gold, platinum, etc.) **39%**
- Base metals and articles thereof **14%**
- Minerals **11%**
- Vehicles and machinery (including transport equipment) **6%**
- Chemicals **5%**
- Agricultural products (animals, vegetables, fruit, fats and oils) **5%**
- Pulp, paper products **3%**
- Textiles, clothing and footwear **3%**
- Prepared foodstuffs (including tobacco) **3%**
- Wood, leather and their products **1%**
- Rubber, plastic and their products **1%**
- Other (including scientific equipment) **9%**

event since John F. Kennedy's funeral in 1963, Nelson Mandela was inaugurated as the first president of a fully democratic South Africa. A crowd of 150,000 watched the event on a giant screen from just outside the buildings.

Wealth and Poverty

South Africa is a curious mix of First World sophistication and Third World underdevelopment. On the one hand it has immense natural resources, employs the latest technologies, supports advanced industrial and commercial structures, and there is a lot of money at the top end of the economic scale. On the other hand, the standard of education among the majority of black South Africans is low; there are too few jobs and services for the rapidly expanding population and the 'poverty cycle', if not quite so horrific as it is in some other African countries, is very real, threatening stability and confusing the decision-making process. What nearly everyone is agreed on, however, is that South Africa's wealth will have to be divided more equitably, the gap between rich and poor narrowed.

How this is to be achieved has been the subject of much debate: organized labour has pushed for central planning within a socialist-type command economy; government and big business favour the creation of wealth (and jobs) through the free play of market forces

The contributions to South Africa's economic wellbeing take no account of the dynamic 'informal economy' that is flourishing and which is partly a product of serious unemployment. The term covers home-based businesses, market trading, hawking, minibus services, crafts and *shebeens* (bars) – a kaleidoscope of mostly tiny ventures which are thought to account for around 30 per cent of total domestic income.

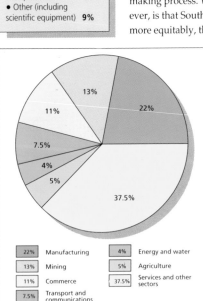

22%	Manufacturing	4%	Energy and water
13%	Mining	5%	Agriculture
11%	Commerce	37.5%	Services and other sectors
7.5%	Transport and communications		

Leading Economic Sectors

These small enterprises have a vital part to play: they provide much-needed work, generate wealth, develop skills and entrepreneurial expertise – and they are helping pioneer the economic future.

Infrastructure

South Africa has an excellent road network that covers the entire country.

Transnet, the nation's semi-private rail undertaking, operates diesel and electric locomotives, carrying 800 million passengers and 200 million tonnes (220,5 million tons) of goods a year. Travel of the most luxurious kind can be enjoyed on the famed **Blue Train**, which plies between Pretoria/Johannesburg and Cape Town, and which has now extended its service to the beautiful Mpumalanga Province.

The main **harbours** are at Durban, Cape Town (Table Bay), Port Elizabeth, Richards Bay, East London (the only river port) and Saldanha Bay. Cargo handling is highly mechanized, storage sophisticated; the bigger outlets have pre-cooling facilities, grain elevators, in-transit warehouses and container terminals.

NATIONAL CENSUS	
The results of the last census, released in 1998, show that South Africa's 40.5 million are distributed among the country's nine provinces in the following percentages of the total:	
KwaZulu-Natal	21%
Gauteng	18%
Eastern Cape	15%
Northern Province	12%
Western Cape Province	10%
North West Province	8%
Mpumalanga	7%
Free State	7%
Northern Cape Province	2%

Below: *Sasolburg's refinery: the world's only viable large-scale oil-from-coal enterprise.*

AGRICULTURE

South Africa is one of the world's few **food exporting** regions, despite generally low rainfall and poor soils (only 12% of the land is suitable for arable farming). A wide range of crops are grown, from **sugar cane** and **subtropical fruits** in KwaZulu-Natal through the **maize** harvests of the North-West to the **tobacco** in Mpumalanga. The national **cattle** herd numbers about 12 million head; some 27 million **sheep** graze the plains of the Great Karoo, Free State and Eastern Cape.

South African Airways, the national carrier, operates a fleet of Boeing 747 and Airbus airliners over a network that spans the globe, and domestic services that cover the main centres. Private airlines serve major, and smaller, towns. There are international airports in Johannesburg , Durban and Cape Town.

Industry

The country's natural resources, added to a vast pool of labour (although this is expensive by the standards of developed countries – productivity is low), technical expertise and political necessity have led South Africa towards industrial self-sufficiency. But the past few years have been a period of painful adjustment for many local industries, hitherto cushioned by protective tariffs and now forced to compete in the global economy. The largest manufacturing sectors are metal products (steel, and everything from cranes and mills to specialized machinery and computer parts); nonmetallic mineral products, vehicles and transport equipment, chemicals and pharmaceuticals, processed foods, clothing and textiles.

Energy

Eskom, the country's power supply utility, produces over 60 per cent of electricity generated on the African continent, exports to neighbouring countries, meets 97 per

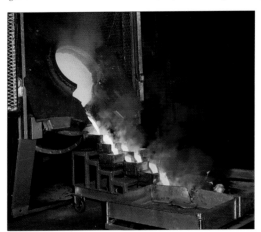

cent of domestic demand, and plans to connect every South African household to the power grid. Coal is the main source, though Eskom also operates **hydro-electric** and **gas-turbine** plants and a nuclear power station. It has also built three huge synfuel plants, which

Left: *Molten gold is poured at the President Brand mine in the Free State.*

supply 35 per cent of domestic needs and represent the world's first and, as yet, only commercially viable **oil-from-coal** enterprise. Viable offshore oil and gas deposits have been located off the south coasts; signs of even larger fields off the western seaboard emerged towards the end of 2000; currently Mossgas, the operating company, produces 30,000 barrels a day, and 1.5 million tons of natural gas and 250,000 tons of condensate a year.

Eskom appears to be on the brink of a landmark breakthrough in the realms of renewable energy technology (**solar power**, at 10 per cent the cost experts hitherto considered attainable) and **nuclear energy** (pebble bed reactors, producing power at around four-sevenths of current cost.

THE PEOPLE

More than a third of South Africa's population of 40.5 million lives in and around the cities and towns, largest of which are Johannesburg, Pretoria and their urban neighbours. Sprawling untidily around every town and city are what used to be called 'African' townships, many of which started life as 'locations' for cheap and temporary labour – makeshift, soulless places in the early days, virtually devoid of civic amenities. Soweto, close to Johannesburg, is the best known. However, urban conditions are improving – the more permanent areas, though grossly overcrowded, have their basic services, electricity, schools, clinics, community centres, sports fields, clubs and shebeens. In some places the streets are paved, and there are pockets of substantial residences – notably in Soweto – for the rapidly emerging African middle class.

But development can't keep pace with the numbers of people driven from a countryside no longer able to support them, and who are lured to the towns by the prospect of jobs and a better life. Vast 'squatter camps' have proliferated

---

MINING

The country has the world's largest known deposits of **gold** (40% of global reserves), **platinum**-group metals (71%), high-grade **chromium** (55%), **manganese** which is vital to the steel industry (78%), **vanadium**, **fluorspar** and **andalusite**, plus massive deposits of **diamonds**, **iron ore**, **coal** (58 billion tons of proven reserves), **uranium**, **nickel** and **phosphates** – nearly 60 commodities in all.

Around 600 tons of gold a year – 40% of the world's total output – is extracted from the mines of the East and West Rand to either side of Johannesburg, and on the giant Free State fields around Welkom.

Below: *At the rock face, drilling the golden seam 2000m (6560ft) below ground. South Africa's mines are among the world's deepest.*

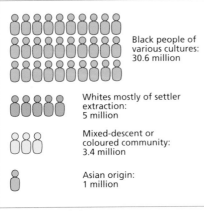

Black people of various cultures: 30.6 million

Whites mostly of settler extraction: 5 million

Mixed-descent or coloured community: 3.4 million

Asian origin: 1 million

South African Population: National Census 1996

NEW ON THE MAP

Many city and town names officially changed at the end of 2000. However the new names are not yet in common currency, and the old ones have been retained in the revised edition of this book. Name changes include:

Pretoria • **Tshwane**
Johannesburg •
City of Johannesburg
Cape Town •
City of Cape Town
Durban •
Durban Metro Unicity
Bloemfontein • **Mangaung**
Port Elizabeth •
Nelson Mandela
East London • **Buffalo City**
Pietersberg • **Polokwane**
Grahamstown • **Makana**
Umtata • **King Sabata Dalindyebo**
Transkei District • **OR Tambo**
Richards Bay • **uMhlathuza**
Nelspruit • **Mbombela**
Graaff-Reinet • **Camdebo**

around the more established townships, densely packed settlements of rudimentary homes, and rows of shelters thrown together with corrugated iron and plastic sheeting. Overall, it's estimated that 700,000 rural folk are migrating to the cities each year, around half the country's population now resides in and around the urban areas, and 'urban drift' – alongside unemployment, the shortage of skills and the AIDS pandemic – ranks among the country's most pressing problems. 'Urban drift', and the need to cope with it, is among the country's most pressing problems.

Language

South Africa's cultural mix is reflected in its confusing variety of languages and dialects. **English** and **Afrikaans** have been the official languages in the past. At present, all 11 spoken languages are official, and the country's most prominent media outlet – the **South African Broadcasting Corporation** (SABC), operates three television channels (SABC1, -2, -3) and numerous regional radio services. There are a number of small, independent radio stations and privately run television channels include **M-Net** (subscription) and **e-tv** (free-to-air).

Religion

Religion is determined largely by cultural origin. Biggest of the **Christian** groups are the Dutch Reformed churches, which have Calvinist roots, followed by the Roman Catholic, Methodist, Anglican, Presbyterian and Baptist congregations. Around 100,000 South Africans are **Jewish**. **Hindus** number nearly 600,000 and **Moslems** 400,000, both concentrated in KwaZulu-Natal, although a large number in the Western Cape also follow Islam.

Combining Christianity with elements of traditional belief are over 2000 indigenous, independent churches,

Left: *A herbalist with the myriad and mysterious ingredients of his trade.*

most of them in the Northern Province and Mpumalanga. Biggest is the Zion Christian Church, which has its own 'city' near Pietersburg in the far north. Most of the groups believe in prophet-healers, and some wear brightly coloured uniforms and robes.

African traditional beliefs – still influential, even among mainstream Christians – are based on a Supreme Being who is infinitely remote from humankind. Lower in the rank is the Inkosi Phezulu – king or paramount chief – and after him, the headman. Last in the hierarchy are ordinary men, women, and children.

Traditional Cultures

Middle-class South African lifestyles, certainly in the towns and their more upmarket suburbs, are virtually indistinguishable from those of any American or European city. Pockets of exotic culture do, however, flourish here and there, and something of the old Africa still survives in the country areas.

Indian society: The country's Asian community, 85 per cent of whom live in and around Greater Durban on the east coast, is a mostly prosperous one that retains the distinctive customs and convictions of the Indian mainland. Lifestyles, certainly among the older generation, are underpinned by the *kutum* – the patriarchal, disciplined extended family that regulates relationships and social interaction. Indian society is strongly unified, but also organized according to the Hindu or Moslem faith, each of which has its own strict rules governing behaviour, manners, food and drink.

The Western Cape's Islamic community: The 'Cape Malays', many of whom are not, in fact, Malaysian at all, but rather descended from slaves brought into the country in the late 1600s from Ceylon and the Indonesian islands of Java, Sumatra and Bali.

TRADITIONAL HEALERS

Diviners, or spirit mediums, play a significant role in traditional cultures. Known to the Zulu as **sangomas**, they are recruited by the ancestors, undergo a rigorous apprenticeship, and act as intermediaries between the living and their forefathers. Techniques vary but, generally, practitioners can predict, divine and heal a multitude of ills, usually of the psychological or social kind.

More down to earth is the **herbalist**, who has filled the role of doctor in traditional village society for centuries, and whose prime function is to cure physical ailments. He (or she) is able to prescribe from a wide range of herbs, tree-bark and other medicinal flora of the veld, many of which are known to have valuable curative properties.

South Africa is a melting pot of cultures and creeds. **Clockwise from top left:** *Mixed-descent (coloured) Capetonian; sari-clad Indian, resident in KwaZulu-Natal; rural Zulu; Afrikaner farmer.*

Some were political prisoners, others high-ranking exiles, and many were skilled craftsmen who, among other things, added decorative charm to early South African architecture. This is a devout, integrated society of around 200,000, which has evolved its own distinctive cuisine and cultural traditions.

Tribal life: European settlement, the drift to the cities and the influence of western culture has destroyed much of the old order, but fragments of traditional Africa have survived. Some **Ndebele** village women still wear heavy anklets and necklaces that can never be removed, and paint the walls of their homesteads in vividly coloured geometric patterns. The **Swazi** of Mpumalanga celebrate unity and the rebirth of their chiefs in a zestful, week-long marathon of dance, song, rituals and endurance tests. **Venda** girls perform the domba snake-dance

to mark their entry into womanhood. **Xhosa** women are famed for their beadwork (the various patterns represent status as well as clan identity), and young Xhosa country boys still go through a long and painful initiation ritual.

Drive through the byways of KwaZulu-Natal and you may see traditional beehive huts made by **Zulu** craftsmen with an eye for beauty. Here, too, are beaded headdresses and the ceremonial regalia of a fast disappearing and perhaps prouder age.

The visual remnants of ancient Africa are everywhere, though it is disappearing fast and much of what remains is especially laid on for the tourist. More resistant to progress are the abstracts – folklore, etiquette and taboo, religion, hereditary rank and the bonds of kinship, concepts of property and land ownership, the nature and obligations of betrothal and marriage. In tribal life, marriages are still arranged by the family and the bride-price, or *lobolo*, is often paid in cows and oxen (the custom is still observed among city dwellers, though hard cash has largely replaced livestock as the appropriate currency).

Sounds of Africa

The African people have a natural gift for rhythm, harmony and spontaneous song. Zulu musical instruments are few and simple – a double-ended cowhide drum, a rattle worn on the ankle or shaken by hand, a reed pipe. But there is also the human orchestra – the powerful, deep-throated roar of men's voices in part harmony, the keening descant of the women, the clapping of hands and the stamping of feet. Other groups create music using xylophones, marimbas and several types of stringed instrument originating from the shooting bow, some with gourds attached to the bow-string for resonance.

Sport and Recreation

South Africa's wonderfully sunny climate is perfect for outdoor life; its people are enthusiastic and, many of them, accomplished sportspersons.

TOWNSHIP JIVE

With the movement to the cities, a new and distinctive sound has emerged. Called **Mbaqanga**, it draws much from the original music of Africa, but has been influenced by American big-band jazz and soul, giving it a vibrant character of its own. Township music defies any simple definition – there are too many ingredients, too many roots – but unmistakable is the throbbing undertone of pure Africa.

Mbaqanga is the African word for maize bread and, like the food it describes, it feeds a deep hunger.

Below: *Marimba player at Cape Town's Baxter Theatre: ancient instruments feature in a great deal of modern South African music.*

FOOD FOR THOUGHT

Biltong: savoury dried meat of Dutch origin.
Bobotie: a light-textured curried meat dish topped with golden savoury custard.
Breyani: spicy Malay or Indian dish prepared with rice and mutton or chicken.
Koeksister: deep-fried, plaited dough, soaked in syrup.
Konfyt: preserve of French Huguenot origin.
Naartjie: a citrus fruit similar to a mandarin or tangerine.
Sosatie: skewered meat and dried apricots marinated in a curry sauce, originating from the Indonesian 'satay'.
Snoek: a firm-fleshed, strongly-flavoured fish, good for smoking and braaiing.
Waterblommetjie bredie: a stew made with indigenous waterlilies.

Below: *Johannesburg's historic Wanderers ground hosts an international one-day cricket match.*

Soccer is king in the African communities, with around 15,000 clubs and nearly a million regular players. Among the leading professional clubs are Kaizer Chiefs, Orlando Pirates, Mamelodi Sundowns, Jomo Cosmos and Moroka Swallows (all in the Johannesburg–Pretoria area), AmaZulu in KwaZulu-Natal and Santos, Hellenic and Ajax Cape Town (all three in the Western Cape). Track athletics, as well as long-distance road-running, are also gaining a large following; world-class runners have already emerged.

Rugby is almost an obsession among many South Africans, and in 1995 the national side (the Springboks) won the coveted Rugby World Cup on its home ground at Ellis Park in Johannesburg. South Africans, too, are passionate about cricket which, as the result of an imaginative development programme, is becoming increasingly popular among people of colour. South Africa will host the Cricket World Cup in 2003.

Hiking, jogging and cycling are sociable and popular recreations. South Africa's more than 400 golf clubs welcome visitors, green fees are reasonable, and most courses are immaculately maintained.

Food and Drink

Special culinary drawcards are the local meat and venison (including springbok, ostrich, kudu and impala), fruit, fish, shellfish – particularly rock lobster (crayfish) –

SUNNY SKIES AND BRAAIVLEIS

The **braai**, one of South Africa's more lasting traditions, is a barbecue featuring well-marinated meats, and spicy **boerewors** ('farmer's sausage'), usually accompanied by beer, wine and a variety of salads. South Africa's sunny climate is perfect for these gatherings, and on weekends tantalizing aromas of sizzling meat fill the air across suburbia.

and other seafood delicacies such as abalone (perlemoen) and oysters. There isn't, however, a single, coherent South African cuisine – the country is too ethnically diverse, and eating patterns are drawn from many different parts of the world. Nevertheless, the eating traditions of some of the immigrant groups – Greek, German, Portuguese, for example – are more prominent than others in various regions. Durban restaurants are renowned for their fiery curries, and marvellous *breyanis*; the Western Cape for traditional fare in which Karoo lamb, venison (particularly springbok pie), sweet potato, cinnamon-flavoured pumpkin and stickily sweet *konfyt* are popular. The Western Cape, too, is the home of 'Malay' cooking, noted for its fragrant *bredies* (a mutton stew with potato, onion and other vegetables), its lightly spiced *boboties* and luscious desserts. The cuisine's origins are mainly Indonesian, though over the centuries other culinary traditions have been influential: curries and samoosas from India; puddings, tarts and biscuits from the early Dutch settlers; the sweet preserves from the French Huguenots. Also part of the South African experience is *potjiekos*, a long-simmering stew created with layers of meat, potatoes and a variety of vegetables in a large cast-iron pot, cooked over an open fire to allow the flavours to mingle.

Traditional African cooking does not appear on many menus. For most of the indigenous people, eating remains a practical and often formidably challenging necessity. The ordinary meal of the day in townships and villages is usually a no-nonsense affair of maize meal ('samp'), vegetables and, less often, stewed meat.

South African wines, both red and white, are generally very good. Some of the labels are fast gaining a reputation for excellence, a generous handful are quite sublime, and many are receiving accolades in international competitions. The wines are still fairly cheap by international standards, though prices have been rising. Some handy and informative volumes on the country's wines can be found in most bookshops.

2
Gauteng and
North West Province

Johannesburg, capital of Gauteng and South Africa's largest metropolis, and **Pretoria**, the country's administrative capital, are located 56km (35 miles) apart on the highest part of the interior plateau known as the **Highveld**. The city was literally built on gold: itinerant workers George Harrison and George Walker stumbled on the Witwatersrand's Main Reef in 1886, and within three years the mining camp of Johannesburg had mushroomed into the country's largest town. **Pretoria**, to the north, is very different in character: older, more sedate, it lies in the warm and fertile valley of the Apies (little ape) River, its eastern suburbs hugging the lovely **Magaliesberg** hills, the central area overlooked by Meintjieskop and the imposing facade of the government's Union Buildings. To the south of Johannesburg lies the enormous urban conglomerate of **Soweto**, and further south is a concentration of industrial towns including Edenvale, Springs and Germiston – the whole come together to form what is now known as **Gauteng** – South Africa's economic heartland.

JOHANNESBURG

Johannesburg has little claim to beauty: to the south, old mine dumps litter the landscape, and the city centre is a concrete-and-glass jungle of high-rises and congested streets. But the city as a whole has its attractions: excellent hotels and restaurants, shopping malls, galleries, museums and theatres, and a vibrancy, an uninhibited zest for life that is reflected on the social as well as the business scene. The surrounding suburbs too, are not

---

CLIMATE

The Highveld has one of the world's most agreeable climates: **summer** days tend to be **warm** and **windless**, but usually end with sudden, heavy downpours. While the winter days are clear the air is crisp and cool, and it is not uncommon for the ground to be covered with frost in the early morning.

Both Pretoria and Johannesburg enjoy an average of nine hours sunshine a day.

Opposite: *Although no gold-mining is done in Johannesburg today, signs of the city's old workings still remain.*

DON'T MISS

*** Sun City and The
Lost City
*** A trip on the Blue Train
*** Gold Reef City
** A tour of Soweto
** Game-viewing in the
Pilanesberg National Park
** A visit to the Randburg
Waterfront complex.

without their own attractions: the green belt along the banks of the **Braamfonteinspruit**, and the many tree-garlanded golf courses are lush areas, and the leafy northern suburbs are pretty. The heart of Johannesburg is in many ways a microcosm of the country; a cultural kaleidoscope of past and future: modern towers are juxtaposed with a few stately survivors of the city's gold-rush days, and pockets of established Portuguese, Indian and Chinese traders jostle with newer African *muti* shops and pavement vendors. Street crime is prevalent, as it is in other big cities of the world, making walking, especially on your own after dark, a risky option.

City Sightseeing

Central Johannesburg, with its density of tall buildings, traffic-congested thoroughfares and crowded pavements , is known as Africa's Manhatten, but there the similarity ends. Most of the larger businesses, department stores, restaurants and bars have moved away to quieter places (notably to chic **Sandton** and other fast developing suburbs to the north) and the street traders have moved in. Still, there's something left for the visitor, especially in the inner-city Hillbrow and Yeoville, and in the ambitious Newtown redevelopment area, where you'll find the Cultural Precinct (centrepiece of which is MuseuMAfrica; *see* page 34) and some exuberant nightlife and 'arts hotspots'.

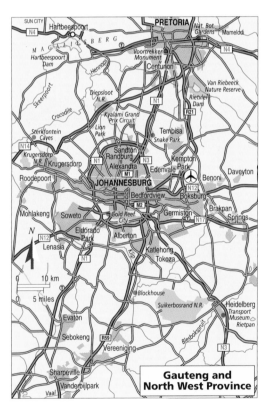

**Gauteng and
North West Province**

Market Theatre Complex ★★

Situated at Mary Fitzgerald Square, this lively complex has four auditoriums, an Indian fruit market, a flower market, clothing and jewellery boutiques, an outstanding second-hand bookshop, bistros – among them legendary **Kippie's Jazz Bar**, designed on the lines of a Victorian public toilet – and live experimental theatre that draws on the African experience.

Gold Reef City ★★★

An evocative reconstruction of pioneer Johannesburg, Gold Reef City is located on the old Crown Mines site, six kilometres (four miles) south of central Johannesburg. The Crown produced 1.4 million kilograms (3.1 million pounds) of gold – worth about US$20 billion at current prices – in its long and honourable lifetime; visitors can descend a mineshaft to explore the underground workings, and watch gold being poured at the museum.

Other attractions are displays of traditional dancing; tram and horse-drawn omnibus rides; a Victorian funfair, pub and tea parlour; replicas of an early theatre, stock exchange, newspaper office; house museums furnished in period style; and many attractive specialty shops (diamonds, leatherware, pottery, glassware, lace, coins,

> ### CITY OF GOLD
>
> Only mountainous dumps and the rusting headgear of the gold mines survive as a reminder of the heady days when Johannesburg (known to the Zulus as *eGoli*, or 'city of gold') was more of a diggers' camp than a city. The industry has moved outwards, to exploit the still-immense wealth of the East and West Rand, and the giant Free State fields. Visits can be arranged through the Chamber of Mines, tel: (011) 498-7100. South Africa's gold output accounts for 40% of the global total. Vaal Reefs is the world's biggest mine; Western Deep Levels is the world's deepest shaft.

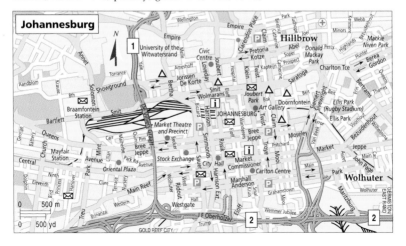

stamps, curios). The **Crown Restaurant** serves gourmet fare; the period-style **Gold Reef City Hotel** offers accommodation from the standard to the luxurious.

Gold Reef City Helicopters will take you on a seven-minute aerial exploration of Johannesburg and Soweto. (Saturday and Sunday from 11:30).

Pick of the Museums and Galleries

MuseuMAfrica, adjacent to the Market Theatre: a treasure house of geological specimens, paintings, prints, photographs relating to the history of southern Africa. **Planetarium (Braamfontein):** explore the wonders of star travel in armchair comfort, including time travel back to the age of the pyramids, Stonehenge and more. Multivisual sky shows Friday to Monday, tel: (011) 716-3199. **Transnet Museum** on the Old Station concourse in De Villiers Street: covers the history of public transport. **Johannesburg Art Gallery (Joubert Park):** offers impressive permanent displays and interesting temporary exhibitions, which include South African, English, French and Dutch works.

Wits Art Gallery in Senate House, Jorissen Street, Braamfontein: displays the Standard Bank collection of African Art; open Tuesday to Friday, 10:00–16:00.

Kim Sacks Gallery (Bellevue): highlights tribal and folk art; open Tuesday to Friday, 10:00–16:00.

Everard Read Contemporary Gallery (Rosebank): showcase mainly for up-and-coming young artists.

OPEN-AIR MARKETS

Regular open-air craft markets are: **Johannesburg flea market**, every Sat in front of the Market Theatre; the **Village Flea Market** in Hillbrow, every Sat and Sun; **Petticoat Lane** in Witkoppen (Victorian gazebo-like stalls in a lake setting), Fri 15:00-21:00, every Sat and Sun; **Organic Market** in Bryanston (cottage industries, natural-fibre clothing, organically grown vegetables, fruits and spices), Thu and Sat, 09:00-13:00. Over the first weekend in each month you can visit **Sandton Collectables** in the Parkview Shopping Centre, and **Artists' Market** at Zoo Lake, an art-and-craft expo; the 700-stall **People's Show** is held every Sat at the National Exhibition Centre near the Crown Mines site.

Theatres and Music

The **Civic Theatre** in Braamfontein is a 1120-seat venue for drama, opera, ballet, light musical productions, orchestral concerts, recitals and other shows; some fine symphonic music can be heard at the **Linder Auditorium** at the Johannesburg College of Education; the **Market Theatre and Precinct**, in the city centre, is an internationally renowned forum for theatre and jazz, and incorporates, among much else, the Foundation for the Creative Arts and the **Newtown Art Gallery**. The visual arts are well represented at, among many other venues, the Everard Read Gallery in Rosebank, the Johannesburg Art Gallery in Joubert Park (central area) and the Goodman Gallery in Parkwood (cuttingedge). For people's music, try the Sakayi nightclub in Rosebank and the Mozambique nightclub in Hillbrow. Gay venues include Therapy and Champions, both in Braamfontein.

Shopping

'World in one' outlets (shops, restaurants, cinemas, and so on) include the **Rosebank Mall** and nearby **The Firs**, just to the north of the city centre; the giant **Eastgate complex**; **Hyde Park Corner**, the Bedford Shopping Centre; and in the northern areas, **Sandton City** and and its neighbour **Sandton Square**, and the **Fourways Mall** in Fourways.

> ### PLANTS AND ANIMALS OF THE CONCRETE JUNGLE
>
> For a breath of fresh air, pay a visit to:
> ** **Florence Bloom Bird Sanctuary** in Delta Park: large variety of species, natural history museum, two small dams with hides.
> ** **Johannesburg Zoo** in Parkview: more than 3000 species of animals, birds and reptiles; for tours, tel: (011) 646-2000.
> ** **Johannesburg Botanical Gardens** in Emmarentia: lovely rose and herb gardens, tel: (011) 958-1750.
> ** **Lion Park** north of the city, on the old Pretoria–Krugersdorp Road: 1-km (half a mile) driving trail.
> * **Lipizzaner stallions** at Kyalami on Sun: book through Computicket.
> * **Melrose Bird Sanctuary** in Melrose.
> * **Transvaal Snake Park** at Midrand.

Opposite page: *Gold Reef City ranks among Johannesburg's leading tourist attractions.*
Left: *Sandton City, mecca for the upmarket shopper.*

Above: *A typical store in downtown Johannesburg.*
Opposite: *Standard housing in Soweto – dull, but fulfilling a vital need.*

MINIBUS TAXIS

During the later years of apartheid rule, boycotts of bus companies and the inadequacies of rail transport gave rise to one of the fastest growing industries the country has ever seen. The need for transport presented an entrepreneurial opportunity and the age of minibus taxis was born. The explosion in the number of these taxis since the 1980s has been phenomenal. They are cheap, fast and sociable, but their safety record is not very reassuring.

Randburg's **Waterfront** is packed with restaurants, bars, cinemas and shops in a two-storey complex surrounding a natural lake, centre of which is a musical fountain with lights. The Waterfront also houses a market, at which some 360 stalls carry crafts and bargains of every description. There is fun for everyone – a playground with a ferris wheel and a carousel for the children, and dancing at four of the restaurants for adults.

Daily markets in and around Johannesburg: **Diagonal Street**, near the stock exchange; **African Market** in the Atrium Centre, Sandton; the **Oriental Plaza** in Fordsburg (an Indian market comprising 275 shops, a must for bargain-hunters). At **Fisherman's Village** on Bruma Lake in Bedfordview are cosmopolitan eating places and boutiques on cobbled, flower-bedecked streets.

Soweto

South Africa's best-known 'black' city (though the demise of apartheid has rendered the term obsolete) straggles across nearly 100km² (39 sq miles) of dusty and unkempt terrain to the southwest of Johannesburg. Much of it is electrified, a growing number of its streets are paved, and the more prosperous residents have large and attractive homes. Formal development has been slow, and the majority of Sowetans live in matchbox houses in over-

crowded conditions which are poorly serviced. There are no high-rise buildings, or flats, to alleviate the situation. Soweto – an acronym of **SO**uth **WE**stern **TO**wnships – was originally designed as a dormitory town. Most workers commute daily by train and minibus to Johannesburg and other nearby centres. Big business has passed Soweto by (until recently it was forced to do so by law), and commercial activity is represented by about 4000 tiny 'spaza' stores and by the burgeoning 'informal sector' (hawking, markets, backyard industries).

Soweto has few civic amenities. The local hospital, **Chris Hani-Baragwanath**, is Africa's largest, while *The Sowetan* newspaper is the country's fastest growing in circulation terms. Social life revolves around the football stadiums and grounds, the myriad *shebeens* (home bars) and the more upmarket nightclubs and community halls. Best way to visit Soweto is with one of the specialist tour operators, biggest and busiest of which is Jimmy's Face to Face Tours (tel: 331-6109), whose excursions depart from selected hotels in Sandton, Rosebank and the central area. There's also Imbizo Tours (tel: 838-2667) whose enterprising owner, Mandy Mankazana, will customize to include nightlife.

UNION BUILDINGS

The splendid crescent-shaped complex of the **Union Buildings**, South Africa's bureaucratic heartland, sits on a hill known as Meintjieskop, from which there are good views of the city and countryside. The neoclassical buildings, designed by the renowned British architect Sir Herbert Baker, were completed in 1913 and served as the model for the larger seat of the Raj government in New Delhi. The beautifully land-scaped grounds are open to the public. Features of note are the **amphitheatre**; the **Garden of Remembrance**; and the **Delville Wood** memorial, commemorating the S.A. Brigade's heroism in the mud of Flanders in July 1916.

THE BLUE TRAIN

South Africa's Blue Train offers the ultimate in luxury travel. The handsome, 16-coach, 107-berth train leaves from Pretoria station, stopping at Johannesburg before heading for Cape Town. Passengers can see some of the country's most spectacular scenery from the elegantly appointed dining car where gourmet meals are served.

For further information, contact Johannesburg Tourism, tel: 784-1352.

PRETORIA

South Africa's administrative capital. Pretoria is a hand-some city, noted for its stately and historic buildings, for its parks and gardens, its splendid wealth of indigenous flora and for its Jacarandas. Some 70,000 of these purple-flowered trees grace the open areas and line about 650km (400 miles) of the city's streets. Pretoria's informal name – the 'Jacaranda City' – derives from their lilac-blossomed glory in springtime (October).

Originally based on the giant Iscor steelworks and the motor industry just to the southwest, Pretoria's industrial sector includes engineering and food processing and, mainly at nearby Cullinan, diamond mining (the 3025-carat Cullinan Diamond – the biggest ever found – was unearthed at the town's Premier Mine in 1905).

The city is also a centre of research and learning. Within and around its limits are **Pretoria University**; Unisa, the world's largest correspondence university; Onderstepoort, an internationally-renowned veterinary research institute; the Medical University of South Africa (Medunsa); Vista University; the Council for Scientific and Industrial Research (CSIR); the Human Sciences Research Council (HSRC); and the South African Bureau of Standards (SABS).

Pretoria is also the headquarters of the South African National Parks, the parastatal organization that manages the country's greatest wildlife areas, including the famed Kruger National Park.

Church Square *

Pretoria became the capital of the independent Boer (Afrikaner) republic of the Transvaal in 1860 and developed mainly around Church Square, the original marketplace and focal point of the isolated Boer community's *nagmaal* (communion), baptisms and weddings. Among the more prominent buildings here are the **Old Raadsaal** (parliament), built in French Renaissance style and completed in 1889, and the graceful **Palace of Justice**. The square's northern frontage is vaguely reminiscent of the Place de la Concorde in Paris, its southern of London's Trafalgar Square (though of course these two places are much grander), and its most striking feature is Dutch sculptor Anton van Wouw's bronze statue of **Paul Kruger**, the 'Father of Afrikanerdom'.

State Theatre **

On its completion in 1981, this complex, comprising five theatres and a public square, was the largest of its kind in the southern hemisphere. Works created by South African artists decorate the open spaces inside the State Theatre. Concerts are often staged on Sunday afternoons; check the newspapers for details.

National Zoological Gardens ***

This is the largest of Africa's zoological gardens, and is home to an extensive array of southern African and exotic animals, including the four great apes, the rare

MONUMENTS TO THE MOVERS

** The **Voortrekker Monument** commemorates the Great Trek – the mass movement of Boers from the British Cape Colony into the interior in the 1830s. It consists of a massive block ringed by 64 granite ox-wagons; one of the two great, decorated chambers inside bears a patriotic inscription commemorating the Boer victory over the Zulus at Blood River in 1838. An impressive monument, but it fits awkwardly into the new South Africa.
** The **Sammy Marks Museum**, on the east side of town, honours one of the previous century's greatest entrepreneurs; **Swartkoppies Hall** is a fine example of Victorian architecture, and opens onto a pleasant tea garden.

Opposite: *Pretoria's neoclassical Union Buildings have long been the headquarters of the country's civil administration.* **Left:** *The streets of Pretoria are lined with exotic Jacaranda trees, earning the city the name 'Jacaranda City'.*

THE GREAT OUTDOORS

For a breath of fresh air, why not pay a visit to:
* * **National Botanical Garden**: more than 5000 indigenous plant species and impressive herbarium.
* * **Jan Smuts House**, Doornkloof, Irene: walk to the great man's grave on a hill with a panoramic view, enjoy tea in the garden afterwards.
* * View of the city from the **Moreleta Spruit trail** in the eastern suburb of Lynnwood Glen; the trail leads through three bird-rich nature reserves.
* **Wonderboom Nature Reserve**, Voortrekker Road: see the 1000-year-old, 23m-tall (75ft) wild fig 'wonder tree'.

TRAILING ARTS AND CRAFTS

The valley of the Crocodile River, about 20km (12miles) northwest of Johannesburg, has attracted an unusual number of talented artists and craftspeople – painters, sculptors, potters, and leather, stone, wood and textile craftsmen. Most of them keep open house on the first weekend of each month. Maps and further information on the **Crocodile River Arts and Crafts Ramble** are available from Gauteng Tourism, tel: 327-2000.

South American maned wolf, a white tiger, and the only known giant eland in captivity in Africa. An aerial cableway takes visitors to the summit of a hill, from where they can view the wildlife. The zoo also contains around 200 different bird species, and there's a fascinating aquarium and reptile park. Carnivores are fed mid-afternoon, seals morning and afternoon.

Pick of the Museums

Kruger House at the corner of Church and Potgieter streets: the modest but charming residence of Paul Kruger (Transvaal President from 1883 to 1900); it has been restored to its original character.

Museum of Culture at the Market Theatre and Precinct: has a fine collection of Cape Dutch and 19th-century furniture, coins, medals and silverware; also archaeology and ethnology exhibits.

Transvaal Museum of Natural History: one-time headquarters of Robert Broom and other celebrated archaeologists; notable are displays of the man-apes, the bird hall, and the 'Life's Genesis' expo.

Melrose House in Jacob Maree Street: an elegant 19th-century home in attractive gardens; the peace treaty of Vereeniging, which ended the Anglo-Boer War in 1902, was signed here.

Pioneer Open-air Museum in Silverton: a Voortrekker farmstead typical of Pretoria's architecture in the 1850s.

SCENIC DAY DRIVES

Hotel Aloe Ridge *

On the West Rand, 45km (28 miles) from Johannesburg, the Aloe Ridge has an adjacent Zulu village, and accommodation in the form of authentic beehive huts. On neighbouring **Heia Safari Ranch**, a South African 'braai' (barbecue) is accompanied by a 'Mzumba' traditional dance drama on Sundays; booking is essential.

Sterkfontein Caves *

To the northwest, in the famed Sterkfontein caves, Dr Robert Broom's excavations yielded a million-year-old

Left: *An Ndebele woman, flanked by the brightly patterned walls of her traditional home in the rural Transvaal region. The women are also renowned for their decorative, finely crafted beadwork.*

fossilized cranium of ape-man *Australopithecus africanus.* The cathedral-like chambers and underground lake are fascinating. Sterkfontein and its neighbouring cave complexes were recently elevated to World Heritage Site status.

Magaliesberg Hills *

To the west of the Johannesburg–Pretoria axis, this ridge has a special woodland beauty all its own and, in the steeper places, even grandeur. Consider staying overnight at the charming Mount Grace Country House or at Valley Lodge, and returning via the **Rustenburg Nature Reserve.**

DeWildt Cheetah Research and Breeding Centre **

This centre, some 30km (19 miles) west of Pretoria, is bound to be a rewarding outing for wildlife enthusiasts. Open on weekends, tours take place at 08:30 and 14:15. Booking is essential.

The Casino Scene

For bright lights, slots, gaming, eating and drinking, there's **Caesar's** in Kempton Park, **Gold Reef City**, the imaginative (Tuscan-style) **Montecasino** in Fourways, **Carnival City** in Brakpan, and **Emerald Safari Resort** in Vanderbijlpark to the south. To north of Pretoria you'll find the **Carousel** and, farther afield (north of Rustenburg), the splendid, older-established **Sun City** complex (*see* pages 42 and 43).

TRADITIONAL LIFE

Tourists interested in traditional African culture and lifestyles should visit the Ndebele village at **Loopspruit**, 55km (28 miles) from Pretoria, which depicts the progression over the centuries of the Ndebele building style.

Nearby is the **Loopspruit Wine Estate**, South Africa's northernmost wine-producing area. Some of these wines have won prestigious awards. Conducted cellar tour, wine tasting and lunch offered.

Exquisite examples of geometrically patterned traditional Ndebele homes and intricately beaded women's costumes can also be seen at the **Botshabelo Museum and Nature Reserve**, near Fort Merensky, 13km (8 miles) north of Middelburg.

There's also the **Mapoch Ndebele Village**, 10km west of the famed **Tswaing Crater** (which is 40km north of Pretoria), and the **Lesedi Cultural Village** (actually four distinctive villages) south of Hartbeespoort Dam.

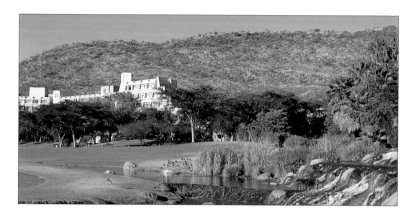

SUN CITY AND PILANESBERG NATIONAL PARK
Sun City★★★

In the North West Province lies an enormous, extravagantly opulent complex of hotels, gaming rooms, theatres, restaurants, bars, discos and shops, all set in spacious and beautifully landscaped grounds: this is the pleasure ground of **Sun City**, flagship of the prestigious Sun International hospitality group and mecca for both local and overseas holiday-makers. In the valley that surrounds Sun City are glittering hotels, ranging from the family-oriented **Cabanas** through the plush, recently refurbished **Sun City** complex and the **Cascades** (whose foyer is cooled by a glistening veil of water spilling down one wall) to the adjacent and magnificent **Lost City** – whose centrepiece is the elaborately domed and minareted Palace Hotel.

THE PALACE OF THE LOST CITY

The **Palace**, an ornate affair of domes and minarets, forms the centrepiece of the multimillion-dollar Lost City development. It has 350 luxurious rooms and suites, two restaurants in fantasy settings of exotic foliage surrounding splendid cascading water features.

The **Valley of Waves**, an outdoor playground, incorporates waterfalls, slides, river rides, a beach and an enormous surf pool with artificially generated waves.

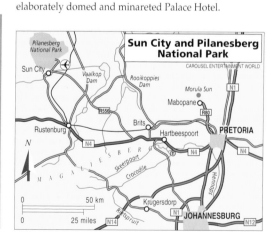

For golfers, there is a choice between the splendid Arizona desert-style golf course where crocodiles lie in wait at the 13th hole, and that at the **Gary Player Country Club**, which has played host to many of the world's greats and is the venue of the annual Million Dollar Golf Challenge.

Among Sun City's other outdoor amenities are riding stables and bowling greens, tennis and squash courts. Much revolves around the various and attractive stretches of water – the waterscape near the Cascades, with its interlinked pools, weirs, tropical walkways and waterfowl; and **Waterworld**, a giant man-made lake designed for both the idle and the water sportsman.

Well worth a visit is the nearby **Kwena Garden**, a 'prehistoric' reptile park and crocodile ranch.

> ### STAYING IN THE PILANESBERG
>
> Accommodation ranges from the luxurious to cottages and caravan facilities. The top private lodges are:
> - **Kwa Maritane**: luxury hotel and timeshare complex situated in the hills; duplex cabanas and chalets with private patios.
> - **Bakubung**: thatched studio rooms and chalets; built around a hippo pool.
> - **Tshukudu**: luxury rest camp set on the crest of a ridge; self-contained chalets.

Pilanesberg National Park**

Sun City is on the southern fringe of the Pilanesberg National Park, a great expanse of game-rich habitat that sprawls within four concentric mountain rings, relics of an aeons-old volcano; at the centre of the bowl is **Mankwe Lake**, which is home to hippo.

Some 10,000 head of game are found in the park, among them both the black and white rhino, giraffe and zebra, lion, cheetah, leopard, brown hyena, elephant, warthog and a wealth of antelope. More than 300 bird species have been identified, and a visit to the **aviary** at Manyane gate should not be missed. The Pilanesberg is traversed by an extensive network of game-viewing roads; conducted walks and drives are available, and viewing hides have been established. Hot-air balloon trips can also be organized.

Opposite: *The lovely gardens of Sun City.*
Right: *The Lost City's Wave Pool: it has a water slide and artificially created waves.*

Gauteng and North–West Province at a Glance

BEST TIMES TO VISIT

Late spring (**September** and **October**) and autumn (**March** and **April**), when skies are usually clear, and temperatures warm.

GETTING THERE

The **international airport** is in Kempton Park, north-east of Johannesburg and southeast of Pretoria, and offers tourist information (Satour JPA), 24-hour banking and currency exchanges, car hire, shopping, restaurant and bar facilities. A regular **bus service** connects the airport with central Johannesburg and Pretoria.

GETTING AROUND

Johannesburg
Best to **hire a car**. City's layout fairly symmetrical – streets and urban freeway system run roughly east–west (M2) and north–south (M1); major routes well signposted and numbered. **Buses** adequate and inexpensive, but are essentially for commuters; regular services operate from around 20 designated areas on city's outskirts. **Taxi cabs** stick to ranks and are pricey.

Pretoria
Pretoria's layout makes detailed map essential. **Airport bus** to Sammy Marks Square in city centre. Hotels offer **courtesy transport**.

WHERE TO STAY

Central reservations
Protea Hotels, tel: 0800 11 9000.
Formule 1, tel (011) 440-1001.
Holiday Inn, tel 0800 11 7711.
Sun International, tel: (011) 780-7800.

Johannesburg
Sandton Sun, Sandton, tel: (011) 780-5000, fax: (011) 780-5002.
Rosebank Hotel, Rosebank. Tel: (011), tel: (011) 447-2700, fax: (011) 447-3276.
The Grace in Rosebank, Rosebank, tel: (011) 280-7200, fax: (011) 280-7474.
Caesar's Palace, Kempton Park, tel: (011) 928-1001, fax: (011) 928-1001.
Sunnyside Park, Parktown, tel: (011) 643-7226, fax: (011)642-0019.
Sans Souci Hotel, Parktown West, tel: (011) 726-6393, fax: (011)480-5983.
Maweni, Protea Golen, Soweto, tel: (011) 986-1142, fax: (011) 986-2119

BUDGET
City Lodge Sandton, tel: (011) 444-5300, fax: (011) 444-5315.
The Cottages, Observatory, tel: (011) 487-2829, fax: (011) 487-2404.
Ah Ha Guesthouse, Bedfordview, tel: (011) 616-3702, fax: (011) 615-3102.
Cooper's Croft, Randburg, tel: (011) 787-2679, fax: (011) 886-7611.

B&B Association (choice of 60 or so establishments), tel: (011) 482-2206 or 803-7170.

Pretoria
Arcadia Hotel, central, tel: (012) 326-9311, fax: (012) 326-1067.
Garden Court Holiday Inn, central area, tel: (102) 322-7500, fax: (012) 47-3597.

BUDGET
La Maison, Hatfield, tel: (012) 43-4341, fax: (021) 342-1531.
Orange Court Lodge, Arcadia, tel: (021)326-6346, fax: (021) 326-2492.
Victoria Hotel, cnr Scheiding and Paul Kruger streets, tel: (021) 323-6052, fax: (021) 323-0843.

Magaliesberg area
Mount Grace Country House, tel: (0142) 77-1350, fax: (0142) 77-1202.
Valley Lodge, tel: (0142 77-1301, fax: (0142) 77-1306.

Sun City
Sun City Hotel, The Cabanas, Cascades Hotel, Palace of the Lost City, Sun International central reservations, tel: (011) 780-7800.

WHERE TO EAT

Johannesburg central
Gramadelas at the Market Theatre, tel: (011) 838-6960. Traditional Cape and African fare.
Kapitan's, tel: (011) 834-8048. Dingy but marvellous curries.

Gauteng and North–West Province at a Glance

Johannesburg north

Ile de France, Cramerview, tel: (011) 706-2837. Superb French provincial food.

Zoo Lake Restaurant, tel: (011) 646-8807. Continental cuisine, pleasant setting.

Linger Longer, Sandton, tel: (011) 884-0465. Renowned chef, French and Eastern fare.

Horatio's Fish Restaurant, Melville, tel: (011) 726-2247. Plain and good.

Osteria Tre Nanni, Parktown, tel: (011) 327-0095. Best of Italian.

Sauselito, Sandown, tel: (011) 783-3305. Very imaginative food and decor;

Gatriles, Sandown, tel: (011) 783-4994. Superb food, award-winning wine cellar.

Johannesburg east

Milky Way Internet Café, Yeoville, tel: (011) 487-3608. What its name suggests.

Gillooly's, Bedfordview, tel: (011) 453-8025. Splendid farmhouse setting.

Johannesburg south and west

Soweto Cappuccino, Orlando West Ext, Soweto. Light meals, excellent coffee.

Edwaleni, Rockville, Soweto, tel: (011)984-7371. Good African hospitality, not too touristy.

Pretoria

Chagall's, Hatfield, tel: (012) 341-7511. Sophisticated; beautiful food, great wine list.

Hillside Tavern, Lynnwood, tel: (012) 47-5119. Splendid steaks.

La Madelaine, Lynnwood Ridge, tel: (012) 44-6076. French-Belgian bistro, voted among top 10.

La Perla, Skinner Street, tel: (012) 322-2759. Seafood a speciality.

Mostapha's, Hatfield, tel: (012) 342-3855. Chef has worked for royalty.

Gerard Moerdyk, Arcadia, tel: (012) 344-4856. Fine South African cuisine.

TOUR OPERATORS

Johannesburg

Ambula Art Safaris, tel: (011) 794-2770.

Bill Harrop's Original Balloon Safaris, tel: (011) 705-3201.

Chamber of Mines (mine tours), tel: (011) 498-7100.

Dumela Africa, tel: (011) 659-9928.

Egoli Tours, tel: (011) 880-4867.

Gold Reef Guides, tel: (011) 496-1400.

Impala Tours, tel: (011) 974-6561.

Jimmy's Face to Face Tours, tel: (011) 331-6109.

Luxliner Tours, tel: (011) 914-4321.

Ma-Africa Tours, tel: (011) 984-2561.

Parktown (heritage) Tours, tel: (011) 482-3349.

Springbok Atlas Tours, tel: (011) 396-1053.

Welcome Tours & Safaris, tel: (011) 286-1607.

Pretoria

City Tours, tel: (012) 347-1000.

Indula Safaris & Tours, tel: (012) 666-7188.

Sakabula Safaris & Tours, tel: (012) 998-8795.

USEFUL CONTACTS

Gauteng Tourism, Rosebank Mall; tel: (011) 327-2000.

Johannesburg International Airport, tel: (011) 975-9963. Information centres at the airport include those of **Satour**, the national tourism body, tel: (011) 970-1669; and **Info Africa**, tel: (011) 390-9000.

Pretoria Tourist Information Centre, Church Square, tel: (012) 308-0839.

Tourism Johannesburg, Village Walk, Sandton, tel: (011) 784-1352.

JOHANNESBURG	J	F	M	A	M	J	J	A	S	O	N	D
AVERAGE TEMP. °C	20	20	18	16	13	10	10	13	16	18	18	19
AVERAGE TEMP. °F	68	68	64	61	55	50	50	55	61	64	64	66
HOURS OF SUN DAILY	8	8	8	8	9	9	9	10	9	9	8	8
RAINFALL mm	131	95	81	55	19	7	6	6	26	72	114	106
RAINFALL ins.	5	4	3	2	1	0.5	0.5	0.5	1	3	4	4
DAYS OF RAINFALL	15	11	11	9	4	2	1	2	3	10	14	14

3
Northern Province and Mpumalanga

About 200km (125 miles) across the great highveld plateau east of the Johannesburg–Pretoria axis, the undulating grasslands give way to hills, and then to mountains that sweep up in an imposing ridge. This is the northern segment of the Great Escarpment that rises near **Nelspruit** and runs north-eastwards for some 300km (185 miles). The Escarpment's eastern faces are especially precipitous, falling to the heat-hazed, game-rich **Lowveld** plain that rolls away across the **Kruger National Park** and neighbouring Mozambique to the Indian Ocean.

THE ESCARPMENT

This is a land of marvellous diversity, a spectacular compound of forest-mantled massifs and high buttresses, sculpted peaks and deep ravines, crystal streams and delicate waterfalls, and of green valleys along which flow the Olifants and Crocodile rivers and their multiple tributaries. The uplands are not as dramatic as their counterparts to the south, the KwaZulu-Natal's Drakensberg (*see* p. 73); on the other hand, they're a lot more accessible to the ordinary traveller: the roads are in good condition, the hotels and hideaways plentiful and inviting.

Blyde River Canyon

Below the confluence of the Treur (sorrow) and Blyde (joy) rivers is one of Africa's natural wonders: a massive and majestic red-sandstone gorge, whose cliff faces plunge almost sheer to the waters below. The 20km-long (12 miles) gorge has been dammed to create a lovely lake;

> **CLIMATE**
>
> Mpumalanga is a summer-rainfall region, where it is generally **hot** in **summer** and very hot in the Lowveld and Kruger National Park. Thunderstorms often occur in the late afternoon, but do not last very long. **Winters** are rather **dry**, while the nights and early mornings very cold on the Escarpment, but milder in the Lowveld.

Opposite: *The Lisbon Falls, near Graskop, is only one of the Escarpment's myriad beautiful cascades. Nearby, Kowyn's Pass offers a spectacular throughway to the Lowveld plain below.*

ESCARPMENT TOWNS

Lydenburg, fly-fishing haven of Mpumalanga, is an attractive and thriving town; the museum, trout hatchery and nature reserve nearby are worth visiting. Higher up the hills is **Sabie**, once a gold town and now centre of the forestry industry (the museum has some fascinating exhibits). Situated on the scenic **Kowyn's Pass** road, is the pretty **Graskop** village. To the southwest is **Dullstroom**, whose railway station is the highest in southern Africa. Dullstroom has two enchanting hotels and a number of nearby luxury lodges. The area is renowned for its trout streams and dams.

at the top of the canyon there are viewing points easily reached from the main road, from which you can gaze across the Lowveld plain and, closer, at the awesome massifs of the Mariepskop and the Three Rondavels.

Much of the countryside around the gorge is occupied by the **Blyderivierspoort Reserve**, known for its diverse plant and bird life (which includes the imposing black (Verreaux's) eagle, and the rare bald ibis which nests on the granite cliffs) – and a fine place for ramblers and horseback riders. Within and just outside the reserve are two pleasant resorts, a reptile park and **Bourke's Luck Potholes**, an intriguing fantasia of water-fashioned rocks.

Perhaps the most breathtaking view site in the entire Escarpment is **God's Window**, a gap in the high mountain rampart near the southern extremity of the reserve.

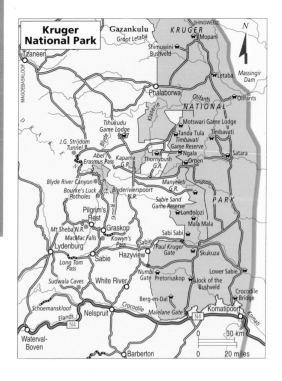

Opposite: *Part of the Blyderivierspoort Nature Reserve, a magnificent upland sanctuary fringing the Blyde River Canyon.*

WATERFALL ROUTE

The unofficial **Waterfall Route** takes in eight waterfalls in the Sabie-Graskop vicinity. The most attractive waterfalls are:

- **Bridal Veil** (aptly named)
- **MacMac** with its twin cataracts; drops into dense ravine, then runs into the exquisite MacMac Pools
- **Lone Creek**, 68m (222ft); and its mist-forest
- **Horseshoe**, a beautiful national monument
- **Berlin** plunges 48m (158ft) into a deep pool
- **Lisbon**, a beautiful twin waterfall.

  Both the Berlin and the Lisbon falls have observation points and picnic sites.

Pilgrim's Rest ***

When gold was discovered on the Escarpment in 1873, diggers flocked in, setting up camps at Spitzkop and MacMac and later – after an even richer strike – at Pilgrim's Rest so-named because, after so many false trails and faded dreams, the gold-hunting fraternity finally found a permanent home here.

The tents and shacks were eventually replaced with iron-roofed cottages, traders set up shop, a church and a newspaper appeared, the **Royal Hotel** opened its doors, and for some years the little frontier settlement flourished. Eventually, though, the alluvial gold ran out and syndicates and companies were formed to dig deeper. The last of the mines closed in the 1970s, although long before then (in the 1940s) the owners had spread their investments, diversifying into timber. Some of the world's largest man-made forests (pine and wattle) now mantle the slopes of the Escarpment.

Pilgrim's Rest still supports a few hundred residents, and its charming early character (1880–1915) has been preserved as a 'living museum'. The Royal still plays host to visitors, and its pub is well patronized. The rooms you sleep in are very much as they were a century

ago. Also available to guests are some of the original miners' cottages, and there are guided tours of the village, of the **Diggers' Museum** (which gives gold-panning demonstrations) and of **Alanglade**, the opulently furnished home of an early mine manager.

SCENIC DAY DRIVES
Panorama Route ★★★

Wherever you go on the Escarpment, you'll find scenic riches and splendid view sites. The circular Panorama Route is especially inviting. Beginning and ending in Sabie, it takes in the MacMac and Lisbon falls, God's Window, the Berlin Falls, a fern-festooned picnic site in the nature reserve, Bourke's Luck Potholes, Blyde River Canyon, the valley of Pilgrim's Creek and Pilgrim's Rest.

Long Tom Pass ★★

Another spectacular escarpment drive winds through **Robber's Pass** and the **Long Tom Pass**. The latter, named after the giant Boer siege-gun that plagued the British during the 1899-1902 war, has especially steep and tortuous gradients. It is notable for its grand vistas, for **The Knuckles** (four peaks in a row) and for **The Staircase**, which defeated many a wagon in the early days.

A drive southwards from Robber's Pass will lead you down a rather steep and rugged track to one of Mpumalanga's finest private nature reserves, **Mount Sheba**. The indigenous forest here is part of an extraordinarily stable floral community that, together with the area's wildlife, forms a coherent ecosystem – and more than 1000 different plant species have been identified here. Paths have been laid out, some leading to old mine workings. Mountain-biking and trout-fishing facilities are also available.

Magoebaskloof ★★

To the northwest, across the Olifants River and on for a further 150km (90 miles), is the attractively tropical farming town of **Tzaneen**, and just beyond, the densely wooded, misty, magical heights of the **Magoebaskloof**. The pass is accessible via a good but very steep road, affording grand views over the surrounding uplands, and the plantations and patches of indigenous forest they sustain.

The loveliest of these is perhaps the Woodbush, which visiting novelist John Buchan described as 'the extreme of richness and beauty'. Woodbush is home to giant yellowwood, ironwood, stinkwood and many other splendid tree species. For cultural and nautural history enthusiasts, both the town of Tzaneen and the nearby Modjadji cycad forest are well worth exploring.

GOING UNDERGROUND

The **Echo complex**, north of Lydenburg, is an intriguing sequence of caverns that echo with disproportionate loudness when you tap their stalagmites and stalactites. The caves were once home to stone-age San, or Bushman peoples; you can see relics of their occupation – rock paintings and excavated sites – at the nearby **Museum of Man**.

More impressive is the **Sudwala system** to the south, a network of caverns thought to burrow through the dolomite for 30km (19 miles) in a series of linked chambers. The nearby **dinosaur park** displays life-sized replicas of the creatures that roamed this part of the earth 240 million years ago.

Left: *Souvenir sellers lend a splash of bright colour to the main tourist routes.*
Opposite: *The main street of Pilgrim's Rest, whose Victorian dwellings have been beautifully preserved.*

Above: *Mpumalanga's tortuous Long Tom Pass was originally built with pick and shovel.*

THE LOWVELD

The low-lying plain below the Escarpment is occupied in large part by the Kruger National Park and bordering private reserves; however an important agricultural industry flourishes around the towns of Nelspruit and White River, in the fertile Crocodile River Valley, where farmlands yield an abundance of subtropical fruits, vegetables and tobacco.

Towns of the Lowveld

Largest of the region's centres, Nelspruit is a prosperous town of wide streets, clean-lined buildings and tree-garlanded suburbs. It's the last major stop on the main west–east highway from Johannesburg and Pretoria.

Among the town's attractions are good hotels and restaurants, sophisticated shops and specialty outlets. Make an effort to visit the **Lowveld Botanical Gardens** on the banks of the Crocodile River, which is known for its fascinating array of local, mainly subtropical plants. Of particular interest – to the layman as well as the botanist – is the herbarium.

To the north of Nelspruit is **White River**, a little country town attractively placed among some of South Africa's richest farming lands: more than 3000 smallholders grow flowers, pecan and macadamia nuts, and subtropical fruits, among other things.

On the other side of Nelspruit, in the steamy De Kaap Valley, lies **Barberton**, yet another South African town founded on gold. The first deposits were discovered in 1883 and, while the reef still yielded its treasure, it was a large and lively settlement – a typical Wild West-type boom town of shanties, music halls, hotels, two stock exchanges and scores of drinking dens. The 'Barberton Bubble' burst soon enough, and the town is much quieter now, but a few hints of the romantic past linger, best seen perhaps in the elegant **Belhaven House Museum**.

KRUGER NATIONAL PARK

Teeming with game, the Kruger National Park and the private reserves that fringe the park's western boundary represent the 'real' Africa. South Africa's premier game sanctuary covers more than 20,000 km² (7720 sq miles) of the Lowveld between the Crocodile River in the south and the Limpopo in the north.

> **THE KRUGER'S 'BIG FIVE' BIRDS**
>
> Almost 500 species of birds have been recorded in the Kruger National Park, including many raptors such as Wahlberg's eagle, bateleur and five species of vulture.
>
> In the rest camps many bird species are habituated.
>
> On your outings, watch out for the following endangered species, which are easily identifiable:
>
> - **Saddlebilled stork**
> - **Lappetfaced vulture**
> - **Martial eagle**
> - **Kori bustard**
> - **Ground hornbill**

Below: *Game-viewing in Kruger National Park; the region is crisscrossed by an extensive network of well-maintained roads.*

FACTS ABOUT THE KRUGER

The park is named after **Paul Kruger**, president of the first Boer Republic, who established the Sabie Game Reserve in 1898. A second reserve (Shingwedzi) was proclaimed in 1903, and the two were combined and renamed the Kruger National Park. **James Stevenson-Hamilton** was appointed as the first curator. A dedicated conservationist (his Shangaan staff called him 'Skukuza' – he who sweeps clean – for his tireless campaign against poaching), the park was elevated to the foremost ranks of the world's wilderness areas during his period in office.

A commemorative trail pays tribute to **Sir Percy FitzPatrick**, a one-time trader who plied the Eastern Transvaal route during the gold rush. His adventures with his dog are immortalized in his famous book *Jock of the Bushveld*.

The park can accommodate around 5000 visitors at any given time; comfort and easy access to the array of wildlife are the keynotes, and there's very little of the classic African safari about your stay here. The rest camps are pleasant, tree-shaded and well-founded oases in a bushveld setting, linked by an extensive network of good roads. Within leisurely driving distance of each camp are waterholes, view sites, picnic spots and a wealth of wildlife and scenic interest.

Fortunately, the Kruger's sheer size ensures that it remains unspoilt. Everything introduced by man – the camps, the designated stopping areas, the routes and the 'visual bands' that run along either side of them – takes up less than three per cent of the area; the other 97 per cent belongs to nature.

The Wildlife

The Kruger National Park boasts the greatest species diversity in Africa, due to the fact that the area encompasses many different habitats. Among the more than 140 resident mammal species are the 'big five': lion (of which there are about 1500); elephant (around 7500); leopard (around 1000 although difficult to spot); buffalo (an impressive 25,000, and which have been seen in herds of up to 200); and rhino, of both the white and black species.

Right: *The Kruger Park's waterholes attract a wealth of wildlife.*

Left: *The Kruger's rest-camps are shady oases in a magnificent wilderness. This is Shingwedzi .*

Rhino are endangered, and especially vulnerable to poaching. Other large game populations include more than 30,000 zebra, 14,000 wildebeest and 5000 giraffe; hippo and crocodile can be seen in numbers in and around the rivers; antelope in their thousands roam the grasslands; and the Park remains one of the few places in South Africa where wild dog can be seen, in the northern reaches of the Park, in its natural environment.

All these forms of life, together with the reptiles and amphibians, the trees (more than 300 species, including baobabs, fever trees, marulas and mopanes; tree lists are available), shrubs and grasses and the uncountable insects and micro-organisms, combine to create a wonderfully coherent habitat, a system of gene pools in perfect (though fragile) balance, and in which the cycle of life is sustained by collective dependence.

The Rest Camps

There are over 20 camps scattered throughout the Park, all pleasant, pretty, clean and safe. Most of the camps are graced by indigenous trees, flowering plants and expanses of lawn. **Bushveld camps** which comprise fully equipped, serviced huts, occur throughout the park, and **private huts** and **chalets** are available on a

---

CREEPY-CRAWLIES

● About a quarter of South Africa's 100 or so snake species can inflict a dangerous bite, among them the adder, mamba, cobra and boom-slang. Snakes tend to avoid confrontation with humans and the likelihood of being bitten is very slight.
● The majority of South Africa's 5000 spider species are harmless; most danger-ous is the button spider, but its bite is rarely fatal.
● Mosquitos present the worst danger in the bush, and the malaria virus that they carry can be fatal.
● Common small red ticks can, if infected, transmit tick-bite fever. The condition is treatable.

Above: *A lioness takes her rest in the mid-day heat. These powerful cats are superb hunters, but drought and disease take a heavy toll, especially among the young.*
Opposite: *Ancient baobab trees feature rather prominently among the Kruger Park's acacia and mopane vegetation.*

block-booking basis. Accommodation is comfortable and spacious: a typical family cottage has two bedrooms including bedding, a bathroom, a toilet, a small kitchen (with refrigerator, stove, utensils, cutlery and crockery provided), a gauzed-in verandah, air conditioning and a barbecue site outside. Lower down the scale are huts without kitchens but communal facilities are available; top of the range are the guest cottages, privately owned but available for hire and, some of them, exceedingly well appointed. Camp routine is relaxed and undemanding, the emphasis on low-cost outdoor living. Visitors usually cook their own meals, although the larger venues have public restaurants – many of which over-look a river or a water hole, or even a well established garden teeming with birdlife.

Daytime game-viewing is done from your own **enclosed vehicle**, along well-signposted routes (maps are available at the Park entrances and shops). All rest camps have set 'gate times' (usually closing at 18:00 and re-opening at 06:00, but this varies from camp to camp and is dependant on the season, so check first). The speed limit in the Park is 40 kph (25 mph) on dirt roads, and 50 kph (30 mph) on tarred roads, so allow for slower speed and time to stop and observe game when working out your time schedules.

Select Camps

Skukuza, the park's headquarters: more of a busy little village than a conventional bush camp. It has all the tourist amenities, including two restaurants, airline and car-hire offices, a supermarket, petrol and service station, a doctor's surgery, an information centre, an exhibition hall, a golf course, and a nursery that sells palms, cycads, baobabs and other indigenous plants. Like most of the other camps, night drives are also offered.

Lower Sabie: located in an area especially rich in wildlife (buffalo, lion and a myriad antelope); has a lovely setting of lawns and shade trees.

Berg-en-Dal: naturally landscaped modern camp (maximum use of local materials has been made); accommodation is well spaced out for privacy; beautiful trees.

Satara: large, with very attractive grounds that are home to a great many birds; the area teems with wildlife. Facilities for night drives are available.

Olifants: sited on a cliff edge, has spectacular views of the game-rich river valley below, and beyond to the hills.

Letaba: very handsome, sited above a sweeping bend in the Letaba River; sundowners on the terrace fill a magical

> ### ON SAFARI: WHAT TO PACK
>
> In the bushveld, nobody dresses up, and most of the **private lodges** have laundry facilities, which means you could probably get away with just a few changes of clothes. Avoid bright colours and white; neutral hues are best for game-viewing and bird-watching. Nights can be chilly, even bitterly cold in winter: pack a warm sweater, tracksuit or anorak. Among other items in your luggage will be a swimming costume, a sun hat, sturdy walking shoes, personal toiletries that include lip salve and sun-protection cream, good sunglasses, insect repellent, malaria prophylactics, a torch, batteries, binoculars, and bird, mammal, insect, plant and tree field-guides.

RAIL SAFARI TO BIG-GAME COUNTRY

Over weekends during the winter months, the luxury **Blue Train** runs between Pretoria and Nelspruit, crossing the scenic route in about six hours. From there, you are whisked off to an exciting game lodge, or you can embark on a tour through the lovely Escarpment area. For information, tel (011) 773-7631/33.

The equally de luxe **Rovos Rail** steam-train excursion, based in Pretoria, undertakes a four-day (return) trip through the spectacular Mpumalanga before descending to the Lowveld, where guests are transported from Komatipoort to the Kruger Park. For information, tel: (012) 323-6052 or (021) 21-4020.

hour. Don't miss out on a visit to the Gold Fields Centre Elephant Museum, which has interesting exhibits.

Mopani: a luxury camp, cleverly designed to blend in with the natural surrounds; offers good views; bungalows are built from stone and thatch.

Shingwedzi: one of the best camps for bird-watchers (keep your eyes peeled for the pearlspotted and African Scops owls and the mourning dove); known for its magnificent elephants.

Punda Maria: northernmost camp; has more than the usual wilderness feel about it; charming and sociable.

PRIVATE GAME RESERVES

The Kruger National Park takes up a large portion of the Lowveld, but by no means all of it. Sprawled along its west–central boundary are, among others, the **Timbavati**, **Manyeleti** and **Sabie Sand** reserves, three of the world's largest private game sanctuaries. Fences between the national park and the private reserves along its western boundary have been removed, and the animals are free to roam over the combined wilderness area. The reserves embrace a score or so luxury game lodges, each with its individual character and special appeal. These are truly

luxurious and include the well–known **Londolozi** and **MalaMala** lodges. The traditional evening 'braai' (barbecue) is memorable; held under the stars, in the firelit, reed-enclosed *boma*, with the night-time sounds of Africa all around, the atmosphere is informal, and the company entertaining, with much talk of wildlife and the bush.

Much of the day is spent in a Land Rover in the company of a ranger–tracker team. The search for spoor is exciting, and the first sighting of game exhilarating. There are also night drives and guided walks.

> ### LUXURY LODGES
>
> • **Inyati**: small, luxurious on the banks of the Sand River.
> • **Londolozi**: ultra-luxurious tree camp, bush camp and main camp.
> • **MalaMala**: top of the range, rated the world's top safari destination.
> • **Motswari** and **M'Bali**: charming rondavels and 'habi-tents' (luxury rooms on a platform).
> • **Ngala**: air-conditioned chalets, en suite bathrooms.
> • **Sabi Sabi**: two camps, one on the river bank, one in the bushveld.
> • **Ulusaba**: two ultra-luxurious lodges, one built on a koppie above the reserve.

Opposite: *The Kruger National Park's secluded Bateleur bush camp.*
Above: *Leopards, the supreme hunters of the wild, thrive in the lowveld.*
Left: *Olifants Rest Camp, set high on a hill.*

Mpumalanga and Northern Province at a Glance

BEST TIMES TO VISIT

Summer in the **Lowveld** very hot and humid; winter days pleasant and sunny (temperatures remain in the 20s), making this the perfect time to visit (**June/July**). Though the countryside is drier, the aloes are resplendent.

The **Escarpment**'s higher altitude ensures a kind climate year-round, though summer brings swathes of mists that affect the views. Best times from **October** to **January**, before the onset of the rains.

Kruger National Park

Winter months (**June** to **August**) are best for game-viewing – trees have lost their leaves, the grass is short, the earth dry, so wildlife tends to congregate around the water holes. In contrast, summer brings life-giving rains, rivers flow, pools fill and bushveld takes on rich luxuriance, but it is also harder to locate and observe wildlife. Towards the end of **November** and **early December**, you will probably see newborns. Malaria is prevalent at this time of the year, so ensure you take the necessary precautions.

GETTING THERE

Nelspruit's **airport** 8 km (5 miles) from centre, with regular flights to and from Johannesburg and Durban. Small **air charters** also operate between airport and various game reserves.

Kruger National Park

By air: Most overseas visitors fly in, either independently or on a package tour. Comair flies direct to Skukuza from Johannesburg; regular scheduled flights from Durban and Johannesburg to Nelspruit and Phalaborwa (Metavia, Air Link). From here, **car hire** services available; minibuses are recommended for game-viewing.

GETTING AROUND

By road: For those who prefer to drive, access routes are excellent; Kruger Park is a comfortable four-hour journey from Johannesburg or Pretoria.

The park has eight entrance gates; petrol outlets at six of them and at larger rest camps. In the interests of safety (yours and that of the animals) travel inside the park is restricted to daylight hours; gates and camps have set opening and closing hours which vary slightly with the season; two camps operate breakdown services. Nelspruit, as the major stop-off point between the Johannesburg–Pretoria and Lowveld–Eastern Escarpment areas, is linked to the major cities by a sophisticated highway system. Very popular tourist venue, especially during school holidays (early **December** to **mid-January**, first three weeks of **April** and most of **July**); advisable to book accommodation well in advance. Reservations can be made through travel agent, or contact **South**

African National Parks, PO Box 787, Pretoria 0001, tel: (012) 343-1991. There is also a regional office in Cape Town, tel: (021) 22-2810.

Pamphlets and brochures describing facilities available; also excellent guidebooks.

WHERE TO STAY

The Escarpment

Mount Sheba, west of Pilgrim's Rest, tel/fax: (013) 768-1241. Luxury hotel and time-share complex, set in exquisite forest reserve.
Blydepoort, perched at the rim of Blyde River Canyon, call Aventura Resorts for reservations, tel/fax: (012) 769-8005. Sweeping views, self-contained chalets and luxury cottages.

Northern Province

Glenshiel Country Lodge, Magoebaskloof, call Country Escapes, tel: (0152) 276-4245, fax: (0152) 276-4475. Gracious, set in rolling hills and meadows.
Troutwaters Inn, Magoebaskloof, tel/fax: (0152) 276-4245. Resort overlooking trout-filled dam.

Trout Fishing Lodges

Bergwaters, Waterval Boven, tel: (013257) 0104. Quiet retreat in Elands River valley, old-fashioned hospitality, country cooking.
Critchley Hackle Lodge, Dullstroom, tel: (01325) 4-0145, fax: 4-0262. Peaceful, stone-built complex at lake's edge, personalized service.

Mpumalanga and Northern Province at a Glance

Dullstroom Inn, in town centre, tel: (013) 764-2292. Reasonable rates, charming pub, tel: (01325) 0017.
Walkerson Country Manor, Dullstroom, tel: (01325) 40246, fax: 40260. Thatch-and-stone manor, views across lake and forest.

Mpumalanga Lowveld
Cybele Forest Lodge, White River, tel: (013) 750-0511, fax: 750-1810. Set in woodland, one of the very best, beautiful rooms, superb cuisine.
Farmhouse Country Lodge, between White River and Hazyview, tel: (013) 737-8780, fax: 737-8783. Thatched luxury suites with magnificent views, lavish farm meals.
Highgrove House, between White River and Hazyview, tel: (013) 764-1844. Colonial-style farmhouse in garden surrounds, breakfast under a gazebo.
Casa do Sol, between Hazyview and Sabie, tel/fax: (013) 737-8111. Mediterranean-style complex of cobbled walkways, archways and fountains.
Jatinga Country Lodge, White River, tel: (013) 751-5059, fax: 751-5072. 1920s homestead with river frontage, candlelight dining.
Old Joe's Kaia, Schoemanskloof Valley, tel/fax: (013) 733-3045. Rustic log cabins in subtropical gardens, lamplit dinners, picknicking at river's edge.
Sefapane Lodge, Copper Street, Phalaborwa, tel: (015)

781-7041. Comfortable 'bee-hive' cottages, poolside bar.
The Rest Country Lodge, 10km from Nelspruit, tel: (013) 741-5011. Luxury suites with balconies and views.

Kruger National Park
For all rest camp accommodation, call **National Parks of South Africa**, tel: Pretoria (012) 343-1991; Cape Town, tel: (021) 22-2810.

Private Game Reserves
Inyati, tel: (011) 880-4469, fax: 788-2406.
Londolozi, tel: (011) 784-7077, fax: 784-7667.
MalaMala, tel: (011) 789-2677, fax: 886-4382.
Motswari/M'Bali, tel: (011) 463-1990, fax: 463-1992.
Ngala, tel: (011) 784-7077, fax: 784-7667.
Sabi Sabi, tel: (011) 483-3939, fax: 483-3799.
Ulusaba, tel: (011) 465-6646, fax: 465-6649.

WHERE TO EAT

Guests at any of the lodges or private game reserves are fully catered for, the cuisine usually excellent. Picnic lunches are

often provided if prior notice is given. Generally, lodges will accept dinner guests not staying at the lodge itself, but reservations are essential. Larger resorts normally have restaurant facilities.

TOUR OPERATORS

Scores of tour companies based in the Johannesburg-Pretoria complex offer excursions to the Escarpment and Lowveld. Local operators include the following (area telephone code 13 in each case): **Hamba Kahle Tours**, 741-1618; **Safari Siligato**, 752-6093; **Sight, Sound and Smell**, 744-7063; **Solitaire Tours and Safaris**, 752-4527; **Vula Tours**, 741-2238; **Lowveld Tours**, 752-6108.

USEFUL CONTACTS

Mpumalanga Tourism Authority, Nelspruit, tel: (013) 752-7001, fax: 752-7001.
Nelspruit Publicity Association/Satour Information, Shop 5, Promenade Centre, tel: (013) 755-1988, fax: 755-1350.
Sondela Tourist Information, Main St, at Old Trading Post, Sabie, tel: (013) 764-3492.

NELSPRUIT	J	F	M	A	M	J	J	A	S	O	N	D
AVERAGE TEMP. °C	24	24	29	21	18	15	15	7	20	21	22	23
AVERAGE TEMP. °F	75	75	84	70	63	59	59	45	68	70	72	73
HOURS OF SUN DAILY	7	7	7	7	8	8	9	9	8	7	6	6
RAINFALL mm	130	119	98	47	19	10	10	10	29	65	114	113
RAINFALL ins.	5	5	4	2	1	0.5	0.5	0.5	11	2.5	4.5	4
DAYS OF RAINFALL	13	12	10	7	4	2	2	2	5	9	13	13

4
KwaZulu-Natal

Known as the 'garden province' of South Africa, KwaZulu-Natal is a well-watered land of rolling green hills and a magnificent Indian Ocean coastline stretching some 600km (370 miles) from Mozambique in the north to the Umtamvuna River in the south. Much of the region's northern half is occupied by the historic territory of **Zululand**; inland, the countryside rises to the foothills and then to the massive heights of the Great Escarpment, here known as the **Drakensberg** (or as legend has it, dragon mountain).

Durban is the province's largest city; **Pietermaritzburg**, in the misty uplands 90km (56 miles) to the west, vies with Ulundi in the heart of Zululand to the north, for provincial capital status. KwaZulu-Natal's predominantly rural economy is based on the vast sugar-cane plantations along its seaboard; other major commodities include tropical and subtropical fruits (pineapples, bananas), dairy products, timber and maize. Coal is mined in the Newcastle area.

Seventy-five per cent of the province's inhabitants are black, mainly **Zulu-speakers**. Some 15 per cent of the population are **Indian**, while **white people** account for the balance of 10 per cent.

DURBAN

South Africa's third largest metropolis, after Johannesburg and Cape Town, and foremost seaport (the harbour is Africa's biggest and busiest and is ranked ninth in the world), Durban began life as the remote trading and white-hunter outpost of Port Natal. Today the city sprawls along

CLIMATE

KwaZulu-Natal's **subtropical** climate is kind to visitors and holidaymakers virtually throughout the year. Rainfall is generous, especially during summer. At this time, the air along the coastal belt is **hot** and **humid** – oppressively so in the weeks around Christmas. Inland, though, the heat usually stays within comfortable limits. Durban enjoys an average maximum temperature in January (high summer) of just over 27°C (81°F) and July (winter) a daily maximum of about 22°C (72°F).

Opposite: *Durban's elegant seafront, mecca for tens of thousands of summertime sun and fun lovers.*

DON'T MISS

*** **KwaZulu-Natal game reserves**: (Hluhluwe-Umfolozi, Mkuzi and Ndumo)
*** **The Drakensberg**: The country's highest mountain range
*** **The Greater St Lucia Wetlands Park**: recently proclaimed a World Heritage Site.

BEST BEACHES

Durban is known for its broad, sweeping beaches, especially those along the **Golden Mile**.

These can be uncomfortably crowded, especially in the weeks before and during the Christmas period, as swimmers, surfers and sun-worshippers flock to the surf. The waters are warm, the rollers often challenging; the shore from **Addington** to **Blue Lagoon** (and many of those beaches further up and down the coast) is protected by shark nets and patrolled by lifeguards and beach constables.

The **Bay of Plenty** on Durban's Golden Mile is the venue for the annual international surfing competition.

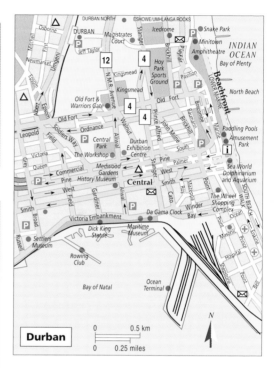

Durban

0   0.5 km

0   0.25 miles

Opposite: Crystal-clear paddling pools on Durban's Golden Mile, a kaleidoscope of gaiety and colour.

the coast to the south, across the Umgeni River in the north, and up and beyond the Berea, a ridge of hills that overlooks the city centre, the beachfront and the bay.

Durban and its subtropical surrounds are among the southern hemisphere's best-known holiday playgrounds, popular for its superb swimming and surfing beaches, its hotels, restaurants and nightspots, its splendid shopping complexes, its surprisingly excellent museums and galleries, its parks and gardens, its sporting amenities, and its lively calendar of social and entertainment events (the imaginative Playhouse complex is perhaps the most notable venue). Much of the attraction lies along the city's famed seafront (*see* opposite) and around its grand harbour. Among other things the latter offers historic Victoria Embankment, its Maritime Museum, and pleasure cruises from Ocean Terminal.

The Golden Mile ★★★

Durban's beachfront, known as the **Golden Mile**, stretches six kilometres (four miles) along the sandy Indian Ocean shoreline and, in addition to the beaches (protected, as are most in and around Durban and the popular resort towns, by anti-shark nets), it offers much to the hedonist: paddling pools, pavilions, piers, amusement parks, colourful markets, and eating places. Apartment blocks and some of the country's best-known hotels line the beachfront boulevard.

Among the strip's special features are the **rickshas**, lightly built carts pulled by Zulu 'drivers', both elaborately decked out in beads, furs and streamers. Today the rickshas survive exclusively as a tourist attraction.

A short walk along the beachfront leads to another wildlife experience – the **FitzSimon's Snake Park** on Snell Parade, North Beach. The park contains a fine collection of exotic and indigenous species plus crocodiles, leguaans (iguanas) and terrapins. Open daily, demonstrations are held four times a day in the bustling tourist season; feeding time for the snakes and crocodiles occurs over the weekend.

Right: *Dolphins go through their paces at Sea World; the impressive oceanarium also features sharks.*

OCEANARIUM

At the bottom of West Street is **Sea World**, one of South Africa's leading marine research centres, and home to the Oceanographic Research Institute. The showcase **aquarium** and **dolphinarium** house a wondrous array of marine fish, stingrays, turtles and sharks, and a fantasia of corals, anemones and seashells. Twice a day divers enter the giant tank to hand-feed the residents.

PEACE AND QUIET

• **Bluff Nature Reserve** in Jacobs: one of Durban's best bird-watching spots.
• **Botanical Gardens** in Lower Berea: indigenous flora, an orchid house and herbarium, and a garden for the blind.
• **Beachwood Mangroves Nature Reserve**, north of Durban: one of the area's last mangrove swamps.
• **Krantzkloof Nature Reserve**: a place of deep gorges, streams, waterfalls and forest; features rare plant and bird species.
• **Umgeni River Bird Park**: rated third among the world's bird parks, with 400 exotic and local species in huge, walk-through aviaries.

At the bottom of West Street is Durban's **Sea World Aquarium and Dolphinarium**, with its bottlenose and dusky dolphins as well as Cape fur seals entertaining throughout the day.

One of Durban's newest shopping complexes is **The Wheel**, a lively collection of speciality shops, restaurants, bars and cinemas in Gillespie Street and Point Road, and **The Bazaar**, which has over 80 stalls offering a wide range of products from leather goods to curios.

For those who need a break from the noise and bustle, take a stroll to the **Amphitheatre** on Marine Parade (opposite the Holiday Inn Crowne Plaza Hotel) – a sunken area of quiet lawns, flowers and fountains, footbridges and gazebos. A colourful flea market is held here every Sunday; traditional dances are performed and exotic dishes served on international theme days.

Access to the Golden Mile can be difficult during the holiday season. The area is packed with people and cars; only the lucky find parking spaces. The best ways to get there from the city centre are by taxi, by conventional bus, by 'mozziecab' (adapted Suzuki jeep), or by the Tuk-Tuk three-wheelers that travel through the city to points along the beachfront. Or make your way there on foot: much of the strip is within comfortable walking distance of the central area – though not in the sweltering heat of a midsummer's day (between December and March).

Shopping

Durban's main shopping area, aside from the Central Business District (CBD), is the imaginative and fun **Workshop**, a large Victorian structure – once the railway workshops – that houses 120 speciality shops (many of them replicas of early colonial houses), barrow stalls and eating places; **The Wheel** on the Golden Mile and **The Bazaar**; **The Arcade**, opposite Pine Parkade, consisting of upmarket speciality shops; and the new **Pavilion** shopping mall (has an Eastern influence) in Westville, 15 minutes out of the city. There are various flea markets – one is in the vicinity of The Workshop, another in the Amphitheatre and yet another on the **South Plaza** of the **Exhibition Centre**.

Right: *Durban city is noted for its unusually wide thoroughfares, of which West Street ranks among the most attractive; it was named after Martin West, first lieutenant-governor of what was then Natal.*

Above: *One of Durban's few remaining rickshas and its decorative 'driver'.*

Museums, Galleries and Theatres

Local History Museum in Aliwal Street: offers a very intriguing insight into Natal's lively past.

KwaMuhle Museum in Ordinance Road: unique (in South Africa) exposition of 20th century urban social history.

Natural Science Museum: houses a life-size model of a dinosaur, an Egyptian mummy, and has an audiovisual display of birds and bird calls.

African Art Centre, off Gardiner Street: a nonprofit enterprise, functions as part shop and part gallery of Zulu arts and crafts, and is housed in the Guildhall Arcade.

Campbell Collections and Centre for Oral Studies: University of Natal, corner of Essenwood and Marriott roads: an eclectic South African culture collection including art, beadwork, books, furniture and paintings.

The Playhouse: a theatre complex (seven auditoriums), its eye-catching decor largely a mix of Tudor and Moorish, reflecting its past as one of the great 'picture palaces'.

North Coast

The upmarket resort area of **Umhlanga Rocks** to the north of Durban boasts fine beaches, luxury hotels, holiday homes and apartments, excellent shops, and more than 30 restaurants. It is known for its safe bathing (particularly to the left of the lighthouse), and excellent surfing. The **La Lucia** residential suburb is one of the region's most fashionable.

The **Dolphin Coast**, quieter than the south, stretches for 90km (55 miles) just north of Umhlanga up to the **Tugela River** mouth. You can travel on either the N2, or the more interesting Old North Coast Road (M4). The old road runs a few kilometres inland, following the trade routes once used by the Zulu *impis*, and now serves the vast plantations and 'sugar towns' of the region, of which **Tongaat** is the 'capital'.

South Coast

Amanzimtoti is a substantial resort town that offers a wide range of holiday accommodation, restaurants, bars, entertainment, marvellous stretches of sand, a lagoon and tidal pool (boats are available for hire), and angling from rock and beach. The is also a tenpin bowling alley at Funland. The nearby **Amanzimtoti Bird Sanctuary**, Umdoni Road, is worth a visit: waterbirds, including the greenbacked heron, are prominent, and peacocks are plentiful; visitor facilities include bird-watching hides, a short walking trail, and cream teas at weekends. The **Ilanda Wilds Nature Reserve** is a small but beautiful and richly varied riverine haven for 160 species of bird and 120 of tree and shrub (there are nature trails and picnic spots). Southwards from Amanzimtoti the coast is lined with scores of little towns, villages and hamlets, each

---

NATAL SHARKS BOARD

The Natal Sharks Board has its headquarters on a hill overlooking the town, and presents fascinating demonstrations three times a week. These include the dissection of a shark, audio-visual presentation and a mini museum; showtimes Tuesday, Wednesday and Thursday at 09:00 and 14.00, Sundays at 14.00. The Board boasts the largest mould of a great white shark in South Africa. Demonstrations are very popular and it is advisable to book in advance, tel: (031) 566-0400.

Below: *The south coast's balmy climate, its golden sands and many charming little resort centres combine to create the most enticing of holiday regions; this is Margate, one of the bigger coastal resorts.*

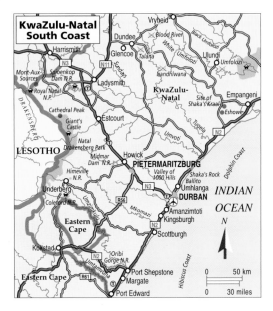

KwaZulu-Natal
South Coast

with its own distinctive charm, most linked by the excellent N2 coastal highway. Prominent among these is **Scottburgh**, which boasts safe bathing, good fishing and **Crocworld**, which includes a complex of crocodile pens, a wildlife museum, a snake pit and a Zulu village where traditional dances are performed on Sunday afternoons.

Port Shepstone boasts one of the country's finest golf courses, and lively **Margate** (the hub of the so-called Hibiscus Coast and focus of annual festivals) offers beaches and a golf course, hotels and self-catering complexes, shops, restaurants and discos.

Inland from Port Shepstone is the **Oribi Gorge Nature Reserve**, a magnificent expanse of rugged hills, deep valleys, emerald grassland and a spectacular canyon, and home of the shy samango monkey; for information, contact the KwaZulu-Natal Nature Conservation Service.

For excitement and glamour, the **Wild Coast Sun** casino resort (*see* p. 89) offers lively round-the-clock entertainment, and is only one and a half hours from Durban, and easily accessible from the South Coast Road.

KwaZulu–Natal Midlands

The main town of the attractive region between the coastal strip and the high Drakensberg is historic and charming **Pietermaritzburg**.

Beyond are the great grassland plains of the KwaZulu-Natal midlands – home to the Zulu nation and scene of bloody 19th-century conflicts between Briton, Boer and Zulu (*see* The Battefields Route, p. 73).

DON'T MISS

** Midmar Dam Resort and Nature Reserve: well-developed area which offers swimming, fishing, boat hire and watersports, a historical village and game-viewing.

The Pietermaritzburg area is famed for its waterfalls:
** Howick: 95m (312ft) high, near the town of that name; designated as a Natural Heritage Site
* Karkloof: has picnic sites
* Albert: surrounded by beautiful countryside

Pietermaritzburg **

A beautiful city of red-brick Victorian buildings, cast-iron store fronts, antique shops, book stores, and of parks and gardens bright with roses and azaleas, Pietermaritzburg was founded by the Boer Voortrekkers in 1838. Its trekker origins can be seen in the **Voortrekker Museum**, formerly known as the Church of the Vow, a small, gabled edifice erected by the Boers to commemorate their 1838 victory over the Zulus at Blood River.

However, the town's history and character are British colonial rather than Afrikaner, its Victorian heritage on display in the **Macrorie House** museum and in the delightful collection of 1850s shops and houses that comprise part of the **Natal Museum** (natural history and ethnology exhibits also draw the eye).

Other reminders of the past include the **Old Natal Parliament**; the magnificent **City Hall**, an imposing affair of domes, stained glass and clock tower (completed in 1900, it's the southern hemisphere's largest all-brick building); and the **Central Lanes**.

This last is a network of narrow alleys that once functioned as the heart of Pietermaritzburg's financial and legal district; of interest here are the small specialty shops and the elaborate Edwardian arcade. Of note is the bronze statue of **Mohandas Gandhi**, unveiled in 1993 to

Below: *The start of the Midmar Mile race, held each year on a massive dam north of Pietermaritzburg.*

commemorate the arrival of Gandhi – known as the Mahatma – in South Africa a century ago. It stands outside the **Colonial Buildings** in the city's Church Street mall.

Valley of a Thousand Hills ***

The region's most striking physical feature is the majestic valley of the Umgeni River between the flat-topped sandstone massif of KwaZulu-Natal's Table Mountain, near Pietermaritzburg, and the Indian Ocean to the east. The area is densely populated in some parts, ruggedly wild in others; the vistas are magnificent, the flora (red-hot pokers, Mexican sunflowers, aloes and, especially, a wealth of lilies) a delight to the eye.

The road that leads along the valley's southern rim is lined with farm and craft stalls and tea gardens; there are also craft studios and shops in and around the small centre of **Bothas Hill** (among them Selkirk's Curio Gallery, The Weavers' Studio next door, The Pottery Studio and The Barn Owl). Some intriguing African art and craft can be seen, too, in the unusual, vaguely Tudor-style **Rob Roy Hotel**, whose terrace is the venue for delicious carvery lunches and cream teas.

If you're in search of the 'authentic' Africa, make a point of visiting **PheZulu**, a 'living museum' village featuring Zulu domestic life, dancing (a pulsating spectacle), bone-throwing, African cooking, thatching, spear-making, an art gallery and a shop. Nearby **Assagay Safari Park** has Nile crocodiles (100 of them), snakes, a natural history museum, curio shop, colonial-style restaurant, and picnic sites. For further information, tel: (031) 777-1208.

THE MIDLANDS MEANDER

This scenically enchanting **arts-and-crafts route** has been established north of Howick, between and around the little villages of **Nottingham Road** and **Lidgetton**. Along the route, studios and workshops offer: weaving, pottery, painting, graphics and art restoration.

The Midlands Meander is one of three routes: the attractions of the **Last Outposts** and the **KwaZulu-Natal Midlands Experience** itineraries also beckon the leisurely sightseer. Check open days with the Publicity Association in Pietermaritzburg or Howick.

Above: *The aptly named Valley of a Thousand Hills, between Pietermaritzburg and Durban.*

Battlefields Route **

For most of the 19th century the Natal midland region was a battlefield, with Zulu, Boer and Briton fighting for supremacy. Military enthusiasts and historians will find the Battlefields Route (including Isandhlwana, Blood River, Rorke's Drift, Ulundi, Majuba Hill, Dundee, Bloukrans, Talana, Elandslaagte, Tugela Heights, Colenso, Ladysmith and Spioenkop) fascinating.

Particularly notable is **Rorke's Drift**, a garrisoned mission station whose British defenders heroically resisted a Zulu onslaught on 1 January 1879; no less than 11 Victoria Crosses were handed out after the engagement. At the **African Craft Centre** at Rorke's Drift, you can view and buy hand-woven rugs and tapestries, handprinted fabrics and fine examples of Zulu pottery. The more important battle of **Isandhlwana**, where the Zulus wiped out a far bigger British force, lies to the east.

One can either book a tour or embark on a self-guided drive around the area; call Pam McFadden, curator of the **Talana Museum**, tel: (0341) 22677, or the local area publicity association for information (a beautifully produced selection of booklets, tapes and brochures is available). An intriguing optional extra for hire is the **Walk 'n Talk** series of tapes (audio commentary plus sound effects as you stroll around).

DRAKENSBERG ***

South Africa's highest mountain range, the Drakensberg is a massive and strikingly beautiful rampart of deep gorges, pinnacles and saw-edged ridges, caves, overhangs and balancing rocks. In the winter months its upper levels lie deep in snow,

Below: *The peaks and buttresses of the Drakensberg, some of which fall sheer for 2000m (about 6500ft), draw climbers from afar.*

CLIMATE

In the Drakensberg, the weather is **highly variable**. Intense heat gives way to extreme cold and, particularly in-summer, to sudden rain-storms. The mountains are prettily clothed in green during the summer, and on **crisp, winter days** the mountain peaks are quilted with snow. Nights are very cold, so remember to take along warm clothing.

but clustered among the foothills far below, in undulating grasslands, is a score of resort hotels, many of them old-established, unpretentious venues created and maintained for the family holiday-maker. People come for the fresh, clean mountain air; for the walks, climbs and drives; for the gentler sports (trout fishing, golf, bowls and horseback riding); and for casual relaxation in the most exquisite of surrounds. Particularly recommended are the **Northern** (the Mont-aux-Sources area) and **Central Drakensberg** (Giant's Castle to Cathedral Peak).

Royal Natal National Park ★★★

This is an extensive floral and wildlife sanctuary, home to antelope and about 200 bird species, among them the black (Verreaux's) eagle, the bearded vulture (lammergeier) and the Cape vulture. Also noted for its scenic magnificence and its 30 or so charted walks, one of the park's longer trails takes you up to the imposing **Mont-aux-Sources** plateau and its **Amphitheatre**; the excursion to **Tugela Falls**, where the river plunges into the pools below in a series of cascades; one stretch drops sheer for 183 metres (600 feet), making it the country's highest waterfall. Horse-riding is popular in the Drakensberg, and numerous bridle paths cross scenically enchanting landscapes. All rides are accompanied by experienced guides. The park's streams and dams offer fine fishing.

TIPS FOR CLIMBERS AND HIKERS

• Don't underestimate the 'Berg: blizzards and storms can descend on the peaks in a matter of minutes. Take warm clothing however balmy the day; don't wear new boots; pack more food than you think you'll need.
• Do your homework: map-reading and route-charting are vital elements of preparation. Note details of your intended trip in the Mountain Register.
• Maps are available from shops of the KwaZulu-Natal Nature Conservation Service.
• Don't venture up on your own: a hiking party ideally comprises three people. Your first outings should be with an experienced hiker/climber.
• Inkosana Lodge in the Champagne Castle area has clearly marked hiking trails suitable for day walks, tel/fax: (036) 468-1202.

Left: *The Sterkspruit Falls is one of the more modest of the Drakensberg's many cataracts and cascades.*
Opposite: *The distinctive Amphitheatre, part of the Drakensberg's Mont-aux-Sources massif, and the Tugela River which plunges down to the Royal Natal National Park.*

Accommodation is available at the Royal Natal National Park Hotel or the Karos Mont-aux-Sources Hotel, as well as at the park's luxury lodge, Tendele. Bungalow, cottage and camping and caravanning accommodation is also available. For reservations and information, contact the KwaZulu-Natal Nature Conservation Service.

Giant's Castle Game Reserve ★★★
Located in central Drakensberg, **Giant's Castle** (part of the larger Drakensberg Park) offers scenic splendour, horseback riding, a stunning array of plant life (a large number of the Drakensberg's 800 flowering species are found here) and a number of raptor species; bearded vultures are fed at hides or 'vulture restaurants', affording visitors the opportunity to study and photograph these majestic birds in their natural environment. The area is dominated by the **Giant's Castle** and **Injesuthi** buttresses. The reserve is famed for its Bushman rock art, some of which is on view in the site museum. Accommodation is available at Giant's Castle camp (lodges, cottages, bungalows and rustic huts) or nearby Injesuthi.

THE ART OF THE ANCIENTS

The Central Drakensberg is remarkable for its rock shelters that long ago served as home to the **Bushman** people, who left traces of their existence in the many rock paintings found around the country. Fine examples of their art can be found in and around the massive **Ndedema Gorge**, where more than 4000 paintings are displayed in 17 'galleries', as well as in the **Giant's Castle** reserve. Together, the two areas hold some 40% of all southern African rock art.

Northern KwaZulu-Natal

Rich and diverse in plant and animal life, Northern KwaZulu-Natal, incorporating the area of Maputaland, boasts some of South Africa's finest game reserves, and one of the world's great wetland and marine sanctuaries.

Maputaland stretches from the Lebombo mountains – up to the Mozambique border and down to the St Lucia estuary – across Northern KwaZulu-Natal and to the sea. This vast wilderness boasts 20 different ecosystems, including three lake systems (including **Lake Sibaya**, South Africa's largest natural freshwater lake, and the **Kosi Bay** lakes with patches of mangrove swamp, and palm and sycamore fig forests).

Opposite: Three young Zulu girls, or intombi, wearing traditional skirts, necklaces, and head- and leg-bands.

Maputaland is the southernmost distribution point for fish and birds, and they are concentrated here like nowhere else in South Africa. Here, off the coast of Northern KwaZulu-Natal in the Maputaland Marine Reserve, coral-encrusted reefs entice the snorkeller, and fishing (even for marlin) is excellent from Black Rock, a 15-minute drive from Rocktail Bay Lodge. For further information, call the KwaZulu–Natal Nature Conservation Service.

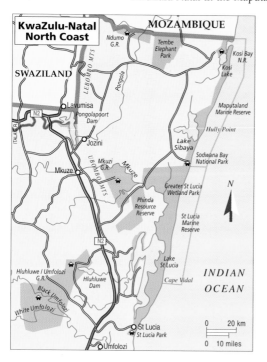

The Greater St Lucia Wetland Park ★★★

From the St Lucia Park north to Sodwana Bay and inland, incorporating Lake St Lucia, is an area comprising an intricate mix of lakes and lagoons, pans, marshland and swamps, sandy forests, palm veld and grassland as well as dunes, beaches and offshore coral reefs – collectively known as **Greater St**

SODWANA BAY

Northern KwaZulu-Natal's offshore coral reefs, the most southerly in the world, are a paradise for scuba divers; especially those at Sodwana Bay. The area is also popular for deep-sea fishing, and offers excellent bird-watching opportunities, and nature trails. A four-wheel-drive vehicle is recommended (a permit must be obtained); diving equipment can be hired. Accommodation is available within the **Sodwana Bay National Park**, at the Sodwana Bay Lodge and Hotel Resort, tel: (031) 304-5977.

Lucia Wetland Park. Centrepiece of this huge conservation area is **Lake St Lucia**, an extensive, shallow estuarine system that teems with waterbirds, and is home to crocodile and hippo. Among the wildlife wonders of the world, gravid sea turtles – loggerheads and leatherbacks – come ashore to lay their eggs on the beaches.

Among visitor amenities are walking trails and excellent opportunities for game-viewing, bird-watching, boating, fishing, scuba diving and snorkelling. Don't miss the Santa Lucia boat tour, which ferries visitors the length of the estuary. The wetland park, which gained World Heritage Site status in 2000, is part of a much bigger scheme – the Lubombo Spacial Development Initiative - which takes in other regional conservation areas (*see* below) together with parts of Swaziland and southern Mozambique.

Maputaland Reserves ★★★

The warm, humid climate and the lush vegatation which support a variety of grasses, shrubs and trees, provide an ideal habitat for a great variety of animals and birds in Northern KwaZulu-Natal. The reserves offer comfortable accommodation, game-viewing roads and walking trails, as well as guided wilderness walks conducted by

ZULULAND

Zulu-speaking people live throughout KwaZulu-Natal. The term **Zululand**, however, is commonly applied to the area stretching north from the Tugela River, the traditional seat of power of the Zulu people. A cultural route offers authentic *kraals* and tangible reminders of past historical battles. Inland, the Nkwaleni Valley is the location of **Shakaland**. One and a half hours from Durban, this complex comprises a hotel in the form of a village of beehive huts. Attractions include Zulu culinary specialities, traditional dancing, displays by *sangomas* (spirit mediums) and herbalists, basket-weaving, pot-making, and hut-building, tel: (035) 460-0912.

Above: *Hikers on the Umfolozi Wilderness Trail stop to study the rugged landscape and its wildlife. The reserve is famed for its rhinos.*

PREVENTION BEFORE CURE

Malaria is endemic to Northern KwaZulu-Natal, and can be contracted throughout the year. Prevention of the disease, which is spread by mosquitos, is vital, as certain infections carry the risk of cerebral malaria which can be fatal. Tablets are available from all pharmacies, and should be taken before visiting the infested area, as directed by the pharmacist.

knowledgeable and competent rangers. Among the more prominent reserves is the **Hluhluwe–Umfolozi Park**. A magnificent area of woodland savanna and flood plain dominated for much of the year by the White and Black Mfolozi rivers in the south, and the Hluhluwe River in the north, the park is a haven for the 'big five', as well as cheetah, giraffe, zebra, blue wildebeest, spotted hyena and wild dog. Famed for its rhino conservation programme, Operation Rhino, begun in the 1960s, the park sustains between 1500 and 2000 white rhinos today.

The northern reaches of the park boast a rich compound of misty forests, grass-covered hills, dense thickets and enchanting rivers. Hluhluwe-Umfolozi sustains 84 mammal species and an impressive 425 bird species. There are splendid accommodation facilities at Hilltop Camp, the exclusive Mtwazi Lodge and the Muntulu Bush Lodge.

Mkuzi is a 34,000ha (84014 acres) sanctuary (part of the Greater St Lucia complex; *see* page 76) comprising savanna, woodland, and riverine forest (giant sycamore figs). The reserve is renowned for its pans, in particular spacious Nsumu Pan, which is haven for a myriad waterbirds. Bird hides have been established. It's also home to hippo, giraffe, antelope and leopard. Accommodation includes a hutted camp and a bush camp.

The **Itala** reserve is located well inland, its northern border running along the banks of the Pongolo River. Its varied wildlife includes black and white rhino, buffalo, giraffe, zebra, antelope, and an array of birds. Ntshondwe Camp has a restaurant and bar, and the luxury lodge offers visitors the opportunity of cooling off in a swimming pool. There are also three attractive bush camps, each of which overlooks water. For further information, contact the KwaZulu-Natal Nature Conservation Service.

Phinda Private Game Reserve, bordering Mkuzi sanctuary, is certainly one of the most upmarket in the country. Home to cheetah and four of the 'big five', Phinda has superbly sited lodges – on mountain, among rocks and in the heart of the riverine forest. For further information, contact the Conservation Corporation, tel: (011) 784-7077.

Ndumo lies in the flood plain of the Pongolo River. The river and pans sustain 400 species of avifauna, among them Pel's fishing owl and the southern banded snake eagle. There are also hippo and crocodile, rhino, giraffe and buffalo, and the shaggy-coated nyala. Accommodation is in a small, attractive hutted camp. **Tembe Elephant Park** has been created to protect the remnants of southern Mozambique's once-great elephant herds. The area is still under development, and while there are few elephants, the park is home to the shy suni antelope and the white rhino. Accommodation consists of three comfortable, tented camps. It is advisable to observe the elephants as part of the organized three-day group expedition. For more information call the KwaZulu-Natal Conservation Service.

PRIVATE LODGES

The region boasts numerous private venues, from the rugged to the super-sophisticated. A few among them:
- **Phinda Private Game Reserve**, at the south end of the Mkuzi reserve: luxury lodges with sweeping views of Ubombo Mountains; superb game-viewing; one of the best ecotourism destinations.
- **Rocktail Bay Lodge**, between Kosi Bay and Sodwana: elevated reed chalets; hippos, crocs and flamingos.
- **Bona Manzi Game Park**, near Hluhluwe: tree-house accommodation.
- **Bushlands Game Lodge**, Hluhluwe: wooden houses on stilts.

Below: *Nyala antelope drink their fill in the Mkuzi Reserve.*

KwaZulu–Natal at a Glance

BEST TIMES TO VISIT

Winter (**June** to **August**) is the best time to visit; tropical heat and high humidity in summer can cause discomfort. Warm Indian Ocean provides pleasant bathing, even in winter.

GETTING AROUND

Durban's **international airport** is 15 minutes from the city centre. A **bus service** operates between airport and city terminal, corner Smith and Aliwal streets. **Car-hire** firms plentiful, and represented at airport; consult hotel reception or Yellow Pages. City **bus** and metered **taxi** services available; phone Eagle Taxis 0800 330 336; Aussie's 0800 323 334; City Taxis (beachfront shuttles) 083 289 0509 and 082 809 3530. Also the mini-cab **Tuk-tuks** (three-wheelers) and 'mozziecabs' (jeeps) for short trips and customized city tours.

WHERE TO STAY

Durban
Royal Hotel, city centre, tel: (031) 304-0331, fax: 307-6884. One of South Africa's oldest, best and most famous.
The Edward, Marine Parade, tel: (031) 337-3681, fax: 332-1692. Elegant, impeccable service.
Holiday Inn Garden Court, Marine Parade, tel: (031) 337-2231, fax; (031) 337-4640.
Tropicana, Marine Parade, tel: (031) 368-1511, fax: 332-6890. On bustling Pedestrian Mall, opposite Sea World.

Four Seasons, Gillsepie Street, tel: (031) 337-3381. Sports bar, seaview rooms.

South Coast
Oribi Gorge Hotel, near reserve, tel: (039) 687-0253. Old-fashioned, good value.
Suntide, Duke Road, Margate, tel: (039) 317-4010. Self-catering apartments.
Windwood Lodge, Palm Beach (Port Edward), tel: (039) 316-8380, fax: (039) 316-8557. Secluded beach location.

North Coast
Beverly Hills Sun Hotel, Umhlanga Rocks, tel: (031) 561-2211, fax: 561-3711. Overlooks beach.
Oyster Box Hotel, Umhlanga Rocks, tel: (031) 561-2233, fax: 561-4072. Gracious.

Pietermaritzburg and Midlands
Imperial Hotel, Pietermaritzburg, tel: (033) 342-6551, fax: 342-9796. Colonial style
Game Valley Lodge, Crammond, tel: (033) 569-0011. Luxurious wildlife getaway.
Wartburger Hof, Wartburg, tel/fax: (033) 503-1482. Country hotel in forest setting.
Tudor Inn, Theatre Lane, central Pietermaritzburg, tel: (033) 342-1778, fax: (033) 345-1030. Small and full of character.
M'sunduzi Lodge, Athlone, Pietermaritzburg, tel and fax: (033) 394-4388. Comfortable B&B (mini-apartments), pool.

Drakensberg
Royal Natal National Park Hotel, Mont-aux-Sources, tel: (036) 438-6200, fax: 438-6101. Colonial-country family resort.
Mont-aux-Sources Hotel, tel and fax: (036) 438-6230. Smart and attractive.
Little Switzerland Hotel mountain resort, between Bergville and Harrismith, tel/fax: (036) 438-6220. Cottages and self-contained chalets.
Champagne Caste Hotel, tel: (036) 468-1063, fax: (036) 468-1306. Pleasantly old-fashioned.
Cathedral Peak Hotel, Winterton, tel/fax: (036) 488-1888. Family resort, great setting.
Drakensberg Sun Hotel, Winterton, tel: (036) 468-1000, fax: 468-1224. In the Cathkin Peak area, superb views.
Sani Pass Hotel, Himeville, tel: (033) 702-1320, fax: 702-0220. Outstanding guest facilities.
Himeville Arms, Himeville, tel/fax: (033) 702-1305. Cosy

Northern Natal
Bonamanzi Game Park, tel: (035) 562-0181, fax: 562-0143.
Bushlands Game Lodge, tel/fax (035) 562-0144.
Phinda Private Game Reserve, tel: (011) 803-8421. Luxury lodges in forest.
Wilderness Safaris, tel: (011) 884-1458, fax: 883-6255.

WHERE TO EAT

Langoustine by the Sea, Durban North, tel: (031) 83-7324. Highlights seafood (prawn curries are excellent).

KwaZulu–Natal at a Glance

Razzmatazz, tel: (031) 561-5847. For the adventurous (porcupine kebabs, zebra pie).
Ulundi in the Royal Hotel, tel: (031) 304-0331. Some of the best Indian food in town.
Aangans, Queen Street, central, tel: (031) 307-1366. Superb Indian food.
Villa D'Este, Davenport & Bulwer roads, central, tel: (031) 202-7920. Seafood and Italian.

TOURS AND EXCURSIONS

Durban city
Historical walkabout, **Durban Experience** and **Feel of Durban** walkabout: Mon–Fri at 09:45, contact Durban Unlimited.
Shuttle bus to and from rickshas, tel: 082 809 3530.
Oriental walkabout: Mon–Fri at 09:45 (visit Victoria Street Market, Juma Mosque, fish market), Durban Unlimited.
Harbour tours: 1-hour boat trip to sea on *Sarie Marais*; regular half-hour harbour tour, contact Durban Unlimited.
Overland and city tours Valley of a Thousand Hills, Shakaland, Wild Coast Sun, Umgeni Bird Park: Exec-U-Tours, tel: (031) 561-5179, fax: 561-4144; Inthaba Tours (in English, Dutch, French and German), tel: (031) 86-6831; Strelitzia Tours (in English, French, German, Italian and Spanish), tel: (031) 86-1904.
Deep-sea fishing, boat charters, helicopter flights, jeep safaris, dolphin viewing, : Blue Dolphin Tourist Service, tel: 082 783

767. Deep-sea fishing, bird-watching, hiking, horseback trails: African Horseback Safaris, tel: (031) 561-4780.
South Coast and Wild Coast Sun: regular excursions depart from the coach terminal at the main railway station; operators include Umhlanga Tours, tel: (031) 561-3777. Helcopters tours: Helcopters Unlimited, tel: (031) 564-0176.
Township tours (informal settlements, Valley of a Thousand Hills), contact Hambe Kahle, tel: (031) 305-5586. Tekweni Eco Tours, tel: (031) 303-1199.

USEFUL CONTACTS

Computicket, theatre/cinema bookings, tel: (031) 304-2753.
Drakensberg Tourism Association, Hotel Walter, Bergville, tel: (036) 448-1557.
Durban Unlimited tourist information, Tourist Junction, 160 Pine Street, Durban, tel: (031) 304-4934; fax: 304-3868.
KwaZulu-Natal Nature Conservation Services (headquarters in Pietermaritzburg) enquiries, tel: (033) 845-

1000, or go to the Tourist Junction, Pine St, Durban.
The Playhouse Company, tel: (031) 369-9555.
Pietermaritzburg Publicity Association, city centre, tel: (0331) 45-1348.
Battlefields Route, tel: (0361) 2830.
Drakensberg Tourism Association, tel: (036) 448-1557.
Durban International Airport, tel: (031) 408-1066)
Durban Museums, tel: (031) 300-6911.
KwaZulu-Natal Golf Union (76 affiliated clubs), tel: (031) 202-7636.
Mozziecabs, tel: (031) 303-6137
Natal Sharks Board, tel: (031) 566-0400.
Tourism KwaZulu-Natal, Tourist Junction, Old Station Building, Pine Street, tel: (031) 304-7144, fax: (031) 304-8792, website: www.tourism-kzn.org
Wildlife and Environment Society, tel: (031) 201-3126.
Zululand Regional Council, tel: (0358) 2-1100.

DURBAN	J	F	M	A	M	J	J	A	S	O	N	D
AVERAGE TEMP. °C	24	25	24	22	19	17	16	17	19	20	22	23
AVERAGE TEMP. °F	75	77	75	72	66	63	61	63	66	68	72	73
HOURS OF SUN DAILY	6	7	7	7	7	7	7	7	6	5	5	6
SEA TEMP. °C	24	25	24	23	21	20	19	19	20	21	22	23
SEA TEMP. °F	75	77	75	72	70	68	66	66	68	70	72	73
RAINFALL mm	135	114	124	87	64	26	44	58	65	89	104	108
RAINFALL ins.	5	4	5	3	3	1	2	2	3	4	4	4
DAYS OF RAINFALL	15	12	12	9	7	5	5	7	10	14	16	15

5
Eastern Cape
and The Wild Coast

The Eastern Cape Province's shoreline extends from the KwaZulu-Natal border at the Umtamvuna River southwards to the Storms River mouth, incorporating previously independent 'homelands' known as Transkei and Ciskei. A varied but entirely beautiful region, the Eastern Cape has a turbulent history. It was here that 19th-century white settler and black tribesman fought long and bitterly for territorial possession, the process of confrontation and conquest starting in earnest with the arrival in Algoa Bay of shiploads of British immigrants – 4000 in all – in 1820.

Despite its strong and obvious colonial past, this area is predominantly the home of the southern Nguni, or Xhosa-speaking people.

PORT ELIZABETH

South Africa's fifth largest city and known variously as the 'friendly city' and the 'windy city' (although it is no windier than many other coastal towns), Port Elizabeth is the economic hub of the Eastern Cape and industrial activity centres around the vehicle-assembly sector. It is also a major tourist centre: set on the shores of Algoa Bay (where the 1820 British settlers landed), it numbers many wide, white beaches, historic buildings, sophisticated shopping centres, and good hotels and restaurants among its drawcards.

Port Elizabeth has four major beaches: **King's, Humewood, Hobie** and **Pollok**. The first comprises long stretches of golden sands, boasts swimming pools, a

CLIMATE

The Eastern Cape straddles the transitional zone between the **'Mediterranean' winter** rainfall and the **subtropical summer** rainfall zones. The air becomes warmer and the summers wetter the further north one travels.

Along the Eastern Cape's Wild Coast the temperature is normally 2C° (4F°) warmer than Port Elizabeth.

Opposite: *The Umtamvuna River marks the boundary between KwaZulu-Natal and the Eastern Cape.*

miniature railway and an entertainment amphitheatre; the second is linked with the sheltered Happy Valley area, which offers level picnicking lawns, beyond which lie quiet lily ponds and shaded riverside paths. Colourful Hobie Beach, flanked by **Shark Rock Pier**, is a popular area for catamaran sailing, rubber-ducking and general beach sports; a thriving flea market crowds the promenade above the sand at weekends. Pollok Beach is a surfer's paradise.

Oceanarium and Museum Complex ***

A visit to Port Elizabeth's **Oceanarium** should not be missed: the dolphins, caught in the bay, are trained to perform for an audience, and Cape fur seals and jackass penguins are quick to join the act.

Notable too are the Aquarium, and the **Snake Park**, one of the country's leading reptile repositories and research centres; the Reptile Rotunda hosts thematic exhibitions; the Tropical House contains colourful bird species and other wildlife in a sculpted landscape of jungle-like vegetation. The **Museum**, housing the Marine Hall, the Bird Hall, the Historical Costume Gallery and a popular children's touch museum, is well worth an hour or two of your time.

JEFFREYS BAY – A SURFER'S DREAM

Less than an hour's drive along the coast west of Port Elizabeth, Jeffreys Bay is renowned for its magnificent surfing rollers (it is the venue of international competitions), for its myriad and enchanting seashells (there's a delightful display in the town's museum), and for its thriving handcraft industry.

Just south of this is Cape St Francis, whose tranquil, unspoilt beaches beckon both sun lovers and surfers.

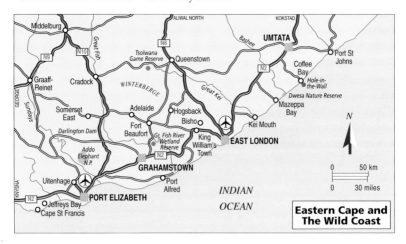

Eastern Cape and The Wild Coast

Nature Rambles

St George's Park, a leafy area with paved walkways, has the country's oldest cricket club and bowling green, swimming baths, an art gallery, and the Victorian **Pearson Conservatory**, whose water lilies are magnificent. On the first Sunday of every month the grounds host **Art in the Park,** a large and lively craft market.

Indigenous flora and an abundance of birds flourish in **Settlers Park**, a unique green belt a stone's throw from the heart of the city, which is best enjoyed from the meandering trail through the Baakens River Gorge (it is advisable that you walk in a group).

Other unspoilt spots around Port Elizabeth offering nature walks (check entry requirements with the Publicity Association beforehand) include: **Island Conservation Area** near Sea View, 15 minutes from town, where the dense indigenous forest yields secretive bushbuck and (among 119 other bird species) the Knysna lourie, and **Van Stadens Wild Flower Reserve**, west of Port Elizabeth: its display of indigenous flowers is a delight from February to August.

Addo Elephant National Park ★★★

The park, just 72km (45 miles) northeast of Port Elizabeth, was proclaimed during the 1930s to preserve the remnants of the once-prolific Cape elephant. The herd, which has the same genetic make-up as the elephants of the Kruger National Park (although only the

---

SAGA OF THE SETTLERS

Tangible evidence of Port Elizabeth's colonial heritage can be seen on the **Donkin Heritage Trail**, described in a booklet obtainable from the Publicity Association.

• **Donkin Reserve**: On his arrival in 1820, Sir Rufane Donkin, acting governor of the Cape, raised a monument to his late wife, Elizabeth, on a hill overlooking the bay, and renamed the settlement after her. The memorial's inscription is a touching tribute. The lighthouse, built in 1861, stands beside the pyramid.

• Around **Market Square** are the City Hall, the old Public Library and St Mary's Collegiate Church (1831); nearby are the restored Railway Station and the Feather Market Hall.

• **No. 7 Castle Hill** (1827), the region's oldest surviving settler home and one of a continuous row of attached houses on the steep hill above the city centre, houses the Historical Museum.

DON'T MISS

★★★ Oceanarium and Museum complex
★★★ Addo Elephant Park
★★ Donkin Heritage Trail, a steep, winding historical walking tour
★★ Grahamstown during the annual Arts Festival
★★ The Wild Coast's unspoilt beaches; stay at the Wild Coast Sun
★ The Eastern Cape's nature hiking trails.

MORE WILD EXPERIENCES

The **Addo Elephant National Park** is destined for rapid expansion in both size and facilities. The process began with the incorporation of the Zuurberg National Park (now known as the **Zuurberg Section**), a major ecotourism venue that offers magnificent mountain scenery as well as an impressive wildlife complement. Nearby is **Shamwari Game Reserve**, a privately owned sanctuary on the Bushmans River and home to a variety of game animals, including the 'big five', in a malaria-free environment. Luxury accommodation is available in a converted Edwardian farmhouse, lodge and two houses. Just south is the **Amakhala Game Reserve**, which hosts giraffe, wildebeest and many kinds of antelope; accommodation in the **Reed Valley** cottages. Much farther away, on the edge of the Winterberg range south-west of Queenstown, is the **Tsolwana Game Reserve**, home to white rhino, wildebeest, mountain reedbuck, ostrich and much else. The enterprise provides funds for the local Xhosa community; overnight visitors have a choice of three luxury Cape-style lodges; on offer are game-viewing drives, horseback trails and, in the evenings, tribal dancing.

males have tusks, which tend to be short), had been reduced to a pitiful 11 individuals, but with careful management their numbers slowly increased to some 200. The park is also a sanctuary for black rhino, buffalo, eland, kudu and other antelope, and about 170 species of bird. Although much of the area is covered by impenetrable thornbush, there are game-viewing roads and viewpoints at the waterholes – where the elephants come to bathe and drink. Night drives offer residents the opportunity to see buffalo and rhino, as well as a number of nocturnal creatures. It is also possible to walk the Spekboom Trail through a 400ha (988 acres) reserve within the park, fenced to preserve the indigenous 'valley bushveld' from elephant, buffalo and rhino. Facilities comprise self-catering chalets and an office, a shop and a restaurant.

GRAHAMSTOWN
The Grahamstown Festival ★★

For an insight into 'state of the art' South African theatre, dance, music, film, fine arts and – increasingly – crafts in South Africa, make sure you don't miss the **National Festival of the Arts** held in July every year and organized by the 1820 Foundation. The venue is Grahamstown, an elegant little centre one and a half hour's drive inland from Port Elizabeth, and a focus of academic and cultural life.

Right: *Elephants in the Addo park; the wild, thickly vegetated terrain is able to support an elephant population three times denser than any other reserve in Africa.*

Known both as the 'city of saints' for the number of its churches (40 places of worship in all) and as the 'settler city' for its British-colonial origins, Grahamstown is home to the prestigious Rhodes University.

Focus of the festival's formal programme is the grandly modern **1820 Settlers National Monument** overlooking the town, where a multitude of venues include a 920-seat auditorium and the vast Memorial Court, whose ornamentation pays tribute to the British contribution to South Africa's cultural heritage. However, for the 10 or so days of the festival, the entire town buzzes with 'fringe' activity, which favours indigenous art and culture. Grahamstown's festival has become a major event on the country's annual social calendar.

Also worth visiting are the **Albany Museum** (the story of the settlers, and African artefacts on display), and the **Observatory Museum** (which features a rare *camera obscura*, a meridian room and diamond exhibition).

Around the Great Fish River

South of East London (South Africa's major river port), the coastline stretches for roughly 65km (40 miles) to the Great Fish River, north of **Port Alfred** (a picturesque resort with a delightful marina and small craft harbour). The estuary of the Great Fish is distinguished by its maze of caves, tunnels and blowholes, and by its birdlife.

Left: *Grahamstown was one of many Eastern Cape villages that started life as a frontier garrison. The city today is characterized by its imposing churches, among them the Anglican cathedral, rising above the town square, and its beautifully preserved early settler and Victorian homes.*

THE LAND OF THE HOBBITS

Northeast of King William's
Town is **Hogsback**, a magical
mountain hamlet comprising
a scattering of permanent
homes, hotels, holiday
bungalows and a shady
camp site, all set above the
exquisite indigenous forests
that provided the inspiration
for J.R.R. Tolkien's *The
Hobbit*. A network of well-
maintained paths leading
alongside streams, past
waterfalls and pools, and
to a huge and ancient tree
provides a paradise for day-
walkers. At the edge of the
forest you can look out over
the plains with their African
settlements far below, from
which voices ring out clearly
in the stillness.

Inland drawcards include two notable nature reserves, of contrasting character and vegetation. Largest and handiest to the coast is the **Great Fish River Wetland Reserve** complex (comprising Double Drift, Sam Knott and Andries Vosloo game reserves), home to hippo, buffalo, black rhino and many antelope species, as well as Bushman (San) rock paintings. The reserve is open to day visitors, but, for those who wish to stay over', comfortable accommodation at a restored Victorian homestead and a private camp is available. **Tsolwana Game Reserve**, a magnificent mountain reserve, incorporates a tribal resource area which earns valuable tourism revenue for the community. Tsolwana hosts a variety of indigenous – rhino, giraffe, wildebeest and springbok – and exotic species – including the Himalayan tahr and fallow deer. The exotics are mainly kept for hunting purposes. Self-catering accommodation is available in farmhouse lodges. Both nature reserves offer walking trails (in the company of trained game guards), wildlife viewing roads, and hunting in season. Permits for visitors to either of these reserves should be pre-arranged through Contour.

THE WILD COAST

Northwards along the Eastern Cape coastline lies the thriving river port of East London, the province's second largest city. Beyond East London lies what was the 'independent' republic of Transkei, with its rugged shore known as the Wild Coast. It is an unspoilt wilderness of beaches and secluded bays, lagoons and estuaries (an impressive 18 rivers find their way to the ocean along this coastal strip), imposing cliffs and rocky reefs that probe, fingerlike, out to sea. Rolling green hills and patches of dense vegetation grace the hinterland.

The **Wild Coast Sun** hotel, casino and resort complex, set beside a tranquil lagoon close to the KwaZulu-Natal border, is a prime tourist destination easily accessible from Durban. A wide range of watersports, a superb golf course, gaming rooms, excellent restaurants, a theatre and two lively show bars are just some of the amenities available to visitors. Other, less flamboyant hotels in quaint towns and hamlets along this coast are more suitable for the leisure-bent visitor: rock, deep-sea, surf and lagoon angling; swimming, surfing, scuba diving (the waters are shark infested though, so take care), or simply revelling in the unspoilt natural surroundings, are just some of the relaxing options. Visitors should be warned, however, that some of the roads to and from these towns are in poor condition, and travelling through these areas is not always safe.

The seaboard's most distinctive physical feature is the **Hole-in-the-Wall**: a massive, detached cliff, with an arched opening through which the surf thunders. A pleasant hour-and-a-half's walk south along the coast from **Coffee Bay** (or an hour's drive – there is no coastal road) will bring you to it. Coastal conservation areas are the small adjoining **Dwesa** and **Cwebe nature reserves,** whose attractions include birds, winding rivers, evergreen forest and a waterfall; accommodation is available. For information and reservations, phone (047) 499-0020.

Opposite: A typical Xhosa homestead in the Eastern Cape. Xhosa women are renowned for the beauty and variety of their beadwork.
Below: *The Hole-in-the-Wall on the Wild Coast is a spectacular detached cliff through which the waves relentlessly pound.*

Eastern Cape and The Wild Coast at a Glance

Eastern Cape coast
Mid-January to **May**; days are warm and almost windless.
Eastern Cape inland
September to **February** (summer); winter too, the snowy mountains are beautiful.
Wild Coast
April to **August** (winter): light breezes and low humidity ensure perfect days, and accommodation rates are low.

Port Elizabeth airport, served by SAA, is 4km (2 miles) from city centre. Hotel transport, taxi (Supercab Shuttle, tel: (041) 457-5590) and car-hire facilities available. **Bisho** and **Umtata** also have airports, but they do not at present feature prominently on the tourism scene. Nearest of the busier airports is **East London's**, served by SAA. **Intercape Ferreira Coaches** link Cape Town with Port Elizabeth and East London; tel: (041) 586-0055.

Port Elizabeth
Car-hire recommended, though metered taxis are on call; the municipal bus service is adequate and cheap; the bus terminus is in Market Square.

East London
Air passengers are served by shuttle bus; city bus service adequate; car-hire facilities available, parking is trouble-free. Coach services (Translux,

Greyhound, Intercape) link the major centres.

Wild Coast
To get to and around the Coast go with a tour operator or on one of the airline package trips. Several Ciskei and Wild Coast resorts have their own airstrips. Driving is not recommended: coastal roads are narrow, with sharp bends, and livestock make them hazardous.

Port Elizabeth
Beach Hotel, Humewood, tel/fax: (041) 583-2161. Close to Oceanarium and Hobie Beach.
The Edward Hotel, Belmont Terrace, tel and fax: (041) 586-2056. Historic building; recently renovated, elegant.
Formule 1 Hotel, Beach Road, tel: (041) 585-6380, fax: (041) 585-6383. Budget; good value.
The Humewood, Beach Road, tel: (041) 585-8961, fax: (041) 585-1740. Family hotel, attractive rooms, attractive bar.
Millbrook House, central, tel: (041) 585-3080, fax: (041) 582-3774. B&B, attractive Victorian home, en-suite rooms.
Protea Lodge, Prospect Hill, tel/fax: (041) 585-1721. Budget, Victorian comfort, self-catering.

Grahamstown area
Settlers Inn, tel: (046) 622-7313, fax: (046) 622-4951. Chalets set in pleasant grounds.
Stone Crescent Hotel, tel/fax: (046) 622-7326. Thatched en-suite huts, mountain views.

The Cock House, Market Street, tel: (046) 636-1295, fax: (046) 636-1287. Victorian country house (one of Nelson Mandela's favoured hostelries)
The Hermitage, Henry Street, tel: (046) 636-1503. B&B, historic home, luxurious suites.

East London
Holiday Inn Garden Court, beachfront, tel and fax: (043) 722-7260. Standard rooms, service and value.
Windsor Cabanas and Windsor Courtyard, near Orient Beach, tel: (043) 743-3220. Mediterranean-style, self-catering an option.

Hogsback
Hogsback Inn, tel: (045) 962-1006. Charming setting.
King's Lodge, tel: (045) 962-1024, fex: (045) 962-1058. For the discerning guest.

Coastal
Fish River Sun Hotel, Ciskei coastal region, tel: Sun International central reservations, (011) 780-7800. Upmarket.
Mpekweni Marine Resort, Ciskei coastal region, tel: Sun International central reservations, (011) 780-7800. Comfortable, family orientated.
Wild Coast Sun, Transkei region, tel: Sun International central reservations, (011) 780-7800. Lavish casino-leisure centre in tropical setting.
Morgan's Bay, Wild Coast, tel/fax: (043) 841-1062. Good food, splendid beach, friendly.

Eastern Cape and The Wild Coast at a Glance

Kei Mouth Beach, Wild Coast, tel/fax (043) 841-1017. Pleasant hotel, sea views.
Trennery's, Qolora Mouth, tel: (047) 498-0004. Atmospheric, very comfortable, nice pool.
Kob Inn, Qora Mouth, tel: (047) 499-0011. Cosy, sociable bar, fine views.

Parks and Reserves
Addo Elephant National Park, for information, South African National Parks, tel: (012) 343-1991. For self-catering cottages.
Shamwari Game Reserve, tel: (042) 851-1224. Private sanctuary, luxury accommodation, big five and other animals.

Port Elizabeth
Aviemore, central, tel: (041) 585-1125. Upmarket, local venison and seafood specialities.
De Kelder, Marine Drive, Summerstrand, tel: (041) 583-2750. Haute cuisine, fine wine-list.
Don Carlos, Russell Road, tel: (041) 585-2828. Family run Spanish, delicious paella.
Le Med, Parliament Street, tel: (041) 585-8711. Unexpected dishes (including Mid-Eastern).
Natti's Thai Kitchen, Clyde St, tel: (041)585-4301. What its name suggests, excellent.

Grahamstown
La Galliera, New St, tel: (046) 622-2345. Italian, very good.
The Cock House, Market Street, tel: (046) 636-1295. Stylish, Provencal dishes.

East London
Movenpick, Orient Beach: superb seafood and other dishes; next-door Quarterdeck.

Recommended is the self-guided **Heritage Walk** around the central area (map available from Tourism Port Elizabeth). There's also the **Sunshine Passenger Service**, tel: (042) 293-191, which offers a customized 24-hour service (minimum 2 passengers). Tourism Port Elizabeth are famously helpful, and will put you in touch with tour operators and their particular interests (game reserves, Bushman rock-art, eco-trailing and so on). Worth a special mention are **Calabash Tours**, which offer a 'Real City Tour' (tel: (041) 585-6162), **Fundani Cultural Tours**, tel: (041) 463-1471 (Frontier War battlefields route), **Tanaqua Indigenous Tours**, tel: 083 270 9924 (hikes and historical excursions); **Pembury Tours**, tel: (041) 481-2581 (big-game, adventure).

Automobile Association, tel: (041) 363-1313.
Bay Tourism, Beach Road (a satellite of Port Elizabeth Tourism), tel: (041) 586-0773.
Country Hospitality East Cape (accommodation bookings, Grahamstown area), tel: (046) 622-8055.
East London tourism information, tel: (043) 722-6015.
Grahamstown Foundation (Festival information and bookings), tel: (046) 622-7115.
Grahamstown tourism information, tel: (046) 622-3241.
South African Airways, Port Elizabeth, tel: (041) 507-1111.
South African National Parks, central reservations (Pretoria), tel: (012) 343-1991
Tourism Port Elizabeth, Donkin Lighthouse, Donkin Reserve, tel: (041) 585-8884
Visitor information (touch-tone service), tel: (041) 586-0773.
Wild Coast Holiday Reservations, tel: (043) 743-6181.

PORT ELIZABETH	J	F	M	A	M	J	J	A	S	O	N	D
AVERAGE TEMP. °C	21	21	20	18	16	14	14	14	15	17	18	20
AVERAGE TEMP. °F	70	70	68	64	61	57	57	57	59	63	64	68
HOURS OF SUN DAILY	9	8	7	7	7	7	7	8	7	8	8	7
SEA TEMP. °C	21	21	20	19	17	16	16	16	17	18	19	21
SEA TEMP. °F	70	70	68	66	63	61	61	61	63	64	66	70
RAINFALL mm	41	39	55	57	68	61	54	75	70	59	49	34
RAINFALL ins.	2	2	2	2	3	2	2	3	3	2	2	1
DAYS OF RAINFALL	2	8	10	9	9	8	8	10	9	11	11	9

6
Garden Route and Little Karoo

The Western Cape coastal terrace running from **Storms River** and the **Tsitsikamma** area in the east to **Mossel Bay**, and inland **Heidelberg** in the west, is known as the Garden Route. It is an enchanting shoreline of lovely bays, high cliffs and wide estuaries with a hinterland of mountains, spectacular passes, rivers, waterfalls and wooded ravines, while the lagoons and lakes around **Knysna** and **Wilderness** are magical. Here you'll find good hotels and eating places; pleasant villages, resorts and marinas; and a warm ocean that beckons bather, yachtsman and angler. Further inland is **Oudtshoorn** and the Little Karoo, a region that has its own special fascination.

THE GARDEN ROUTE
Tsitsikamma Area

The **Tsitsikamma National Park** embraces an 80km-strip (50 miles) of superb coastline together with a marine reserve that stretches five kilometres (three miles) offshore. The land area is richly endowed with plant life and birds; the rock pools teem with colourful marine life; and whales and dolphins can often be seen sporting close to the shoreline. The forest reserve's indigenous trees include the giant yellowwoods, which can grow to over 50m (165ft); among these is the famous 'Big Tree', estimated to be over 800 years old. Within the park there are various nature walks winding through beautiful forests and along the scenic cliffs. For adventurous swimmers and divers, there is an underwater trail.

Opposite: *The rugged cliffs of The Point at Cape St Blaize, near Mossel Bay. Whales and dolphins can often be seen sporting in these waters.*

Right: *The resort centre at the mouth of the Storms River which rises in the Tsitsikamma mountains.*
Opposite: *The hotel complex on Plettenberg Bay's Beacon Island flanked by golden sands.*

The park is also traversed by the popular five-day **Otter Hiking Trail**, which leads through 41km (25 miles) of unsurpassed coastal scenery from **Storms River Mouth** to **Nature's Valley**, a charming village in a setting of mountain, forest, lagoon and sea.

Visitors to the Tsitsikamma area can spend a night in the fully equipped oceanettes, cottages or chalets at the Storms River Mouth rest camp (the beautiful surrounds make this a popular stopover). For more information, contact the National Parks of South Africa.

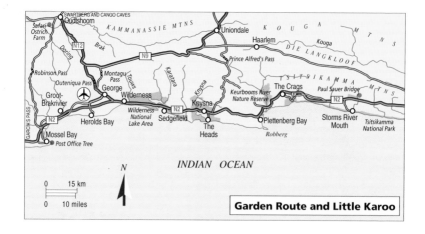

Garden Route and Little Karoo

Plettenberg Bay

'Plett', as it is known colloquially by South Africans, is one of the country's most fashionable holiday resorts. The town's amenities include country inns, holiday cottages, restaurants, shops, boutiques and bars, and **Beacon Island**, which supports a large and sophisticated hotel and time-share complex set on fine golden sand. There are facilities for golf, bowls, horse riding, angling, scuba diving, boating and sailing.

The nearby **Robberg** and **Keurbooms River** nature reserves attract ramblers and bird-watchers.

Recommended picnic excursions include those to the **Kranshoek** lookout point and picnic site, part of the Harkerville State Forest, and to the **Garden of Eden**, where many of the trees are labelled.

Knysna

Knysna, also a popular resort centre, is celebrated for its fresh oysters and fine hardwood furniture. The biggest drawcards are the **Knysna Lagoon** guarded by two cliffs known as **The Heads** and the new **Waterfront** complex.

The lagoon, popular among boating enthusiasts, water-skiers and fishermen, harbours a variety of fish and waterbirds, crabs, prawns, 'pansy shells' and the very rare sea horse (*Hippocampus capensis*). Cabin cruisers and houseboats can be hired; the **John Benn**, a 20-ton pleasure boat, offers sightseeing, live entertainment, wining and dining); booking essential.

WHAT TO SEE AND DO IN KNYSNA

- **Millwood Museum**: displays of local history, gold mining, timber industry.
- Try fresh oysters at Knysna Oyster Co. or lunch at Jetty Tapas on **Thesen's Island**.
- Visit the Norman-style church and historic guesthouse at **Belvedere**.
- Stroll past the five **castles** on the sea at **Noetzie** (note, these are private residences).
- Enjoy the art and crafts at **Die Ou Fabriek**, in the garden of Craft House. Also **Bitou Crafts**: spinners, weavers and knitters at work.

TRAIN IT

The **Outeniqua Choo Tjoe** is a Class 24 narrow-gauge steam train that plies between **George** and **Knysna**, crossing the spectacular Kaaimans River bridge to run through lovely wooded country, along the shoreline and over the lagoon. The journey takes just over three hours, and you will have time to enjoy a pub lunch before the return trip (excursions Mon to Fri, and Sat during the Christmas season). To book a seat on the train, tel: (044) 382-1361 or 801-8288, or contact the reservations office of the local publicity association.

GEORGE

Largest of the Garden Route towns, it nestles at the foot of the high **Outeniqua Mountains**. George is the aerial gateway to the region.

Worth visiting in and around town are the **George Museum**, noted for its fine array of antique musical instruments and exhibits relating to the timber industry; and the local **crocodile park**, a small breeding farm which is also rich in birdlife. Fishing, bathing and sun worshipping are all good at **Herolds Bay** and at secluded **Victoria Bay**, both nearby.

Residents at the Fancourt Hotel can play golf at the exclusive **Fancourt Country Club** estate's 27-hole golf course, designed by veteran golfer Gary Player.

Nearby, tennis, bowling, horse riding, hiking, squash and watersport facilities are available.

The eastern Head has a fine view of Knysna, its lagoon and **Leisure Island** (an attractive residential complex); on the western Head is the **Featherbed Nature Reserve**. Free access to the reserve is by boat. There are guided excursions along **Bushbuck Walk**.

Knysna Forest, together with the Tsitsikamma Forest woodlands to the east, form South Africa's largest expanse of indigenous high forest: a 36,400ha (89,940 acres) home to giant yellowwood, stinkwood and other indigenous trees. The **Diepwalle Forest Station**, off the R339, is the starting point for the **Elephant Walk**, some 20km (12 miles) in total (there are shorter routes) through this impressive forest.

Wilderness Lakes Area

Wilderness is an enchanting little seaside resort to the west of Knysna, set around a lagoon which is the first in a chain of 'lakes' that lie between the two towns.

The wider Wilderness area, administered by the National Parks of South Africa, embraces five rivers, 28km (17 miles) of coastline and six large bodies of water: the **Wilderness Lagoon**, the **Serpentine**, **Island Lake**, **Langvlei**, **Rondevlei** and **Swartvlei**.

The many aquatic plants, as well as the sedge and reed beds provide food and shelter for fish and for about 200 species of bird, including 80 different species of waterfowl.

The Wilderness area is very popular among holidaymakers; Swartvlei and Island Lake are favoured by water sportsmen, and the whole region by ramblers, hikers, bird-watchers and anglers. Rondevlei and Langvlei – where you can see fish eagles, ospreys, herons and kingfishers – both have bird hides. Accommodation in Wilderness is available in several good hotels, holiday cottages and National Parks chalets.

Below: *Sandstone 'heads' flank the sea entrance to Knysna's lovely lagoon.*

Mossel Bay

Since the discovery and exploitation of offshore oil deposits, Mossel Bay has grown considerably. Steeped in history, it is a popular holiday destination.

In long bygone times the area was home to the Khoikhoi people, labelled 'Strandlopers' (beach walkers), by early Dutch seafarers and settlers; their staple diet of mussels gave the bay its name. It was also known to Portuguese who preceded the Dutch in their exploration of the southern African coast. Admiral João da Nova built a small stone chapel on the shores (nothing remains of this); Bartolomeu Dias, Vasco da Gama and others filled their ships' casks from the perennial spring and 'posted' letters and documents in the trunk of a large milkwood tree (which is known as The Post Office Tree today) for collection by the next passing fleet. Something of this rather intriguing past can be seen in the town's **Bartolomeu Dias Museum**.

Also of interest is **Seal Island**, home to around 2000 of these marine mammals (cruises start from the harbour), and **The Point**, from which you have a spectacular seascape view (whales and dolphins can sometimes be seen).

THE LITTLE KAROO AND OUDTSHOORN

Contrasting sharply with the lush coast, this distinctive region with its own, harsher beauty, sprawls between the **Outeniqua** and **Langeberg** mountain ranges and the grand **Swartberg**. The flattish plain below these uplands is part of the Karoo system, but is very different from the

SCENIC MOUNTAIN PASSES

Several scenic and historic roads lead off the Garden Route to cross the various mountain ranges. Among the most impressive is the **Swartberg Pass**, 24km (15 miles) of stunning views between Oudtshoorn and Prince Albert, on the fringes of the Great Karoo. Equally attractive are the **Bloukrans** and the **Grootrivier passes**, in the Tsitsikamma area; **Prince Alfred's Pass** between Knysna and the Longkloof; **Montagu Pass** between George and Herolds Bay; the **Outeniqua Pass** between George and Oudtshoorn; **Robinson Pass** between Mossel Bay and Oudtshoorn; **Garcia's Pass** between Riversdale and Ladismith in the Little Karoo; and **Seweweekspoort** (Seven Weeks Pass) – described as one of the 'scenic wonders of the world' – through the Swartberg.

Left: *The vintage Class 24 locomotive, known as the Outeniqua Choo-tjou, puffs its way across the Kaaimans River estuary.*

OSTRICH FACT FILE

An ostrich lives for up to 40 years. The adults are plucked every nine months or so, yielding a kilogram of feathers each time. These are used mainly in the manufacture of fashion accessories and household dusters, but the bird is also exploited for its meat (in the form of 'biltong' and ostrich steaks – an increasingly popular delicacy); for its egg (equal in bulk and nutrition to 24 hen's eggs); and for its skin (handbags, wallets, belts and shoes).

Below: *The riding of ostriches is cause for much hilarity among visitors to Oudtshoorn's show-farms.*

Great Karoo wilderness that lies beyond the Swartberg. It is not a high rainfall area, but is watered by the many streams that flow down from the mountains, and the land yields rich harvests of wheat, emerald-green lucerne, tobacco, grapes and walnuts.

Oudtshoorn

The Little Karoo's main town, set on the banks of the Grobbelaars River, was (and still is) the focal point of the ostrich industry, which had its heyday during the fashion-led ostrich-feather boom in the late 19th and early 20th centuries. Reminders of this time can still be seen in one or two ostentatious 'feather palaces', built by the wealthy farmers and traders of yesteryear.

Visit the annex of the **C. P. Nel Museum** for its Ostrich Room and antique collection. Other surviving mansions include **Dorphuis**, **Pinehurst** and, outside town, **Greystones** and **Welgeluk**. Among the ostrich show-farms are the worthwhile **Highgate** and **Safari**. Both offer guided tours during which you are shown all facets of the ostrich business, and you are given the opportunity to watch the birds going through their paces on the race-track (these are known as 'ostrich derbys').

If you are adventurous enough, you can even choose to ride astride one yourself. For a quicker, more intensive tour, call in at the **Cango Ostrich Farm**. Visitors in more leisurely mode can take the **Ostrich Express** through the Little Karoo to Calitzdorp; you're shown around a wine estate, treated to dinner and entertainment and then returned by rail the next morning.

Above: *An illuminated chamber in the giant Cango Caves; not all the labyrinths have been charted.*

Cango Caves ★★★

This labyrinthine complex of caverns, in the Swartberg range some 25km (16 miles) north of Oudtshoorn, is ranked among the most remarkable of Africa's natural wonders. The 28 chambers of Cango One (the first of the sequences to be charted) are linked by over two kilometres (one mile) of passages, and contain a marvellous fantasia of weirdly sculpted, many-coloured stalagmites and stalactites. It takes about two hours to walk this route, but elderly people, or those who are a little less energetic, need not complete the full tour. Biggest of the caves is the Grand Hall, 16m (53ft) high and 107m (350ft) across. Among the more interesting dripstone formations are the 'Organ Pipes', 'Cleopatra's Needle' and the 'Frozen Waterfall'. The caves are open daily; there are conducted tours (every hour on the hour in peak season, every two hours at other times), a restaurant and a curio shop. Call the Oudtshoorn Publicity Association for further details.

CANGO WILDLIFE RANCH

Situated 3km (2 miles) from Oudtshoorn, on the way to the Cango Caves, this farm has over 400 **Nile crocodiles** and a handful of **American alligators**, and a unique complex where Africa's largest cats can be observed in their natural environment. A raised walkway through natural bushveld allows visitors to watch and photograph **cheetah, lion** and the three rare white **Bengal tigers**. The walkway leads to a train which takes you through a deer park to the fully licenced Zindago's restaurant. Open daily all year round from 08:00. Guided tours are conducted throughout the day. Tel: (044) 272-5593 to book.

Garden Route and Little Karoo at a Glance

A mild, equitable climate makes it a pleasant destination all year round. Highest rainfall (though not excessive) in **August** and **September** (late winter). Busiest during **December** school holidays.

The Garden Route's main **airport** is 10 km (6 miles) from George. Regular flights by SAA from South Africa's major cities. The main N2 highway (Cape Town to Port Elizabeth and beyond), which takes motorists along the Route, is in excellent condition. Coach services operate from Cape Town, George airport and Port Elizabeth.

An excellent network of roads links the Garden Route's main centres. Major car-hire firms are represented at George airport and throughout the region.

Tsitsikamma / Storms River
Tsitsikamma Forest Inn, Storms River, tel: (042) 541-1711, fax: 541-1669. Set in the foothills, lovely views.
The Old Village Inn, Tsitsikamma, tel: (042) 541-1607, fax: 541-1629. Cape-style hotel complex.

Plettenberg Bay
Hunter's Country House, tel: (044) 532-7818, fax: 532-7878. Exclusive thatched retreat overlooking indigenous forests.
The Plettenberg Hotel, tel: (044) 533-2030, fax: 533-2074.

Elegant, international reputation, on a cliff with sea views.
Stromboli's Inn, mid-way between the Bay and the Wilderness lakes, tel: (044) 532-7710, fax: (044) 532-7823. En-suite lodges set in pleasantly shady grounds.
Bayview Hotel, central, tel: (044) 533-1961, fax: (044) 533-2059. Modern, well appointed.
La Vista Lodge, tel: (044) 533-3491, fax: (044) 533-5065. En-suite rooms, fine views over Keurbooms lagoon; two golf courses in area.

Wilderness
Fairy Knowe Hotel, tel: (044) 877-1100, fax: 877-0364. Quaint thatched rondavels and riverside rooms, wide range of watersports.
Karos Wilderness Hotel, tel: (044) 877-1110, fax: 877-0600. Excellent quality, sandwiched between forest and sea.
Far Hills Protea, tel: (044) 871-1295 or call Protea Hotels toll free 0800-11-9000. Country hotel at the foothills of the Outeniqua Mountains.

Knysna
Gallery Guest House, tel: (044) 382-2510, fax: 382-5212. Colonial-style home, fine balcony views.
Knysna Protea Hotel, tel/fax: (044) 382-3568. Luxurious, efficiently run.
Point Lodge, tel: (044) 382-1944, fax: 382-3455. Lakeside, owner-managed, friendly, tranquil setting.

Leisure Isle Lodge, on Ballard Bay, tel: (044) 384-0462, fax: (044) 384-1027. Top-rated guesthouse, superb views.
Yellowwood Lodge, tel: (044) 382-5906, fax: (044) 382-4230. Owner-managed, friendly, nice rooms, fine views of lagoon.

Mossel Bay
Old Post Office Tree Manor, tel: (044) 691-3738, fax: 691-3104. Part of historic stone museum complex at site of ancient milkwood tree where Portuguese navigators left messages 500 years ago.
The Point Hotel, tel: (044) 691-3512, fax: (044) 691-5315. Luxurious sea-facing rooms with private balconies.
Highview Lodge, tel: (044): 691-9038, fax: (044) 690-6628. Mix of self-catering and full service, fine views of harbour.

George
Fancourt Hotel and Country Club Estate, tel: (044) 870-8282, fax: 870-7605. Elegant, stylish, golf course for exclusive use of hotel guests.
Hoogekraal Country House, tel: (044) 879-1277, fax: 879-1300. Gracious homestead dating back to 18th century.

Oudtshoorn
Kango Protea, tel: (044) 272-6161, fax: 272-6772. Thatched rondavels in farm-like setting.
Rosenhof Country Lodge, tel: (044) 272-2232, fax: 272-2260. Restored Victorian house, herb and rose-filled gardens.

Garden Route and Little Karoo at a Glance

Budget Accommodation
Holiday Inn Garden Courts:
Wilderness, tel: (044)
877-1104, fax: 877-1134.
Oudtshoorn, tel: (0443)
22-2101, fax: 22-2104.

Where to Eat

Plettenberg Bay
Stromboli's Inn, Knysna and
Plettenberg Bay, tel: (044)
532-7710. Fine country dining.
The Islander, 8km from town,
towards Knysna, tel: (044) 532-
7776. Fabulous seafood buffet.
**Bothers Restuarant &
Terrace**, Main Street, tel:
(044) 533-5056. Appealing
decor, breakfasts and lunches.
Cornuti al Mare, tel: (044)
533-1444. Splendid Italian fare.

Knysna
Oyster Tasting Tavern,
Thesen's Jetty, Thesen's
Island, tel: (044) 382-6941.
Sample the finest seafood.
Knysna Hollow Restaurant,
on country estate near town,
tel: (044) 382-5401. Discerning
menu, nicely prepared dishes.
Brenton Beach Restaurant,
tel: (044) 381-0081. Lovely
views, a la carte and buffet.
The Anchorage, tel: (044)
382-5553. Old-established,
nautical decor, mainly seafood.

Mossel Bay
The Gannet, Bartolemeu Dias
Museum complex, tel: (044)
691-1885. Mainly seafood.
Jazzbury's, tel: (044) 691-
1923. Local and ethnic specialities (inc mopane worms).

George
The Copper Pot, tel: (044)
870-7378. Old homestead,
Cape bistro menu.
Alte Feste, tel: (044) 884-
0707. Seafood, grain-fed beef
dishes, decadent desserts.

Oudtshoorn
**Bernard's Taphuis-
Restaurant**, tel: (044) 272-
3208. Country cuisine (down-
stairs), bar meals (upstairs).
Jemima's, tel: (044) 272-
0808. Eclectic menu, mostly
dishes of the region.

Tours and Excursions

Eco-marine trips (plus para-
sailing) from Plettenburg Bay,
Ocean Safaris, tel: (044) 533-
4963. **River adventure**
(with walking trails, picnics),
Keurbooms Rover Ferries, tel:
(044) 532-7876. See the **Big
Five** and cultural village,
whale & dolphin watching,
river cruises, tel: (044) 532-
7710. **Ecotorism**: Ecobound
Tours & Travel, (044) 801-
8239. **Adventure**: Adrenaline
Connection, (044) 871-1286.

Horseback trails, hikes in
Zuurberg/Addo area, tel: (042)
233-0583. The Little (Klein)
Karoo **Wine Route** invites
exploration (see brelow).
Flower Route (Southern
Cape Herbarium, George): tel:
(044) 874-1558. **MTN Whale
Route**, tel 0800 228 222.

Useful Contacts

Accommodation, Garden
Route central reservations, tel:
(044) 874-7474/0067.
**Garden Route Tourism
Office**, tel: (044) 873-6314/55
George Tourism Bureau,
tel: (044) 801-9295
Knysna Tourism Bureau,
tel: (044) 382-6960.
**Little (Klein) Karoo Tourism
Office**, tel: (044) 272-2241.
**Little (Klein) Karoo Wine
Route**, tel: Oudtshoorn (044)
279-2532, and Calitzdorp, tel:
(044) 213-3312.
**Mossel Bay Tourism
Bureau**, tel: (044) 691-2202.
**Oudtshoorn Tourism
Bureau**, tel: (044) 279-2532.
**Plettenberg Bay Info
Centre**, tel: (044) 533-4065.

MOSSEL BAY	J	F	M	A	M	J	J	A	S	O	N	D
AVERAGE TEMP. °C	21	21	20	18	17	16	15	15	15	16	18	20
AVERAGE TEMP. °F	70	70	68	64	63	61	59	59	59	61	64	68
HOURS OF SUN DAILY	7	7	7	7	8	8	8	7	7	7	7	7
SEA TEMP. °C	22	22	20	19	18	16	16	16	16	17	19	21
SEA TEMP. °F	72	72	68	66	64	61	61	61	61	63	66	70
RAINFALL mm	28	31	36	40	37	31	32	36	39	38	34	28
RAINFALL ins.	1	1	1.5	1.5	1.5	1	1	1.5	1.5	1.5	1	1
DAYS OF RAINFALL	7	7	8	8	8	7	7	8	8	9	8	6

7
Western Cape Province

Cape Town's metropolis huddles in the 'bowl' that is formed by majestic **Table Mountain**, its flanking peaks and the broad sweep of **Table Bay**. Suburbs and satellite towns sprawl across the low-lying **Cape Flats** and southwards over much of the scenically beautiful **Cape Peninsula**.

Inland are the grand mountain ranges and fertile valleys of the Cape Winelands, contrasting with the rugged, windswept West Coast (having its own special beauty) and, beyond, bleak **Namaqualand**, which is transformed in spring with vast, sweeping fields of brilliantly coloured wildflowers.

South Africa's oldest city, Cape Town was founded by the first Dutch settlers who, led by Jan van Riebeeck, landed on the tip of Africa in April 1652. Set beneath the grandeur of Table Mountain, the area was described by English circumnavigator Sir Francis Drake as 'the fairest cape in all the circumference of the earth'. The harbour is quieter than it was in the heyday of the great Union-Castle passenger liners, but a part of the waterfront has been imaginatively redeveloped for tourism, plenty of ships still call, and marine and mercantile industries contribute much to the local economy.

Among the top attractions are the wide choice of eating and drinking places, excellent hotels, craft markets and speciality shops, a lively calendar of arts, superb beaches, Kirstenbosch National Botanical Gardens, Table Mountain and the cableway and the Peninsula's unique mountain and coastal scenery.

CLIMATE

The Western Cape coast has a **Mediterranean** climate, receiving winter rainfall. The **long summer days** (December, January, February) can be blisteringly hot, but towards the end of the year are usually disturbed by a gusty **southeaster** (known as the 'Cape doctor' because it clears away the city smog) that may last for days and can reach gale force. The **winter** months (May, June, July) are **cold** and **wet**, and the inland mountains are often snow-capped.

Opposite: *Table Mountain, viewed from Milnerton. The massif on the right is Lion's Head.*

DON'T MISS

*** A cable-car ride to the
top of Table Mountain
*** Sundowners at the
V & A Waterfront
*** A visit to scenic
Stellenbosch and winelands
** Tea at Kirstenbosch
National Botanical Gardens
** A tour of the historic
Groot Constantia Estate
** A day at glittering Canal
Walk, the hemisphere's
largest shopping centre.
** Exploring the Public
Gardens and South
African Museum
* Bargain-hunting on
Greenmarket Square.

Opposite: *Table Mountain*
viewed from Signal Hill.

CAPE TOWN
Table Mountain ★★★

This is Cape Town's premier attraction. The mountain
rises 1086m (3564ft) above sea level and there are magnificent views from its distinctively flat-topped summit.
Often, though, the heights are mantled by clouds and in
summer, driven by the strong 'southeaster' wind, they
tumble over its precipitous northern face to form a spectacular 'tablecloth'. At the top there are short walks, a
licensed restaurant and a souvenir shop. You can reach the
summit on foot along one of several charted paths; some
are easy, others difficult – and the mountain, despite warn-
ings, regularly takes its toll of human life. Arm yourself
with a good map or climb with someone who knows the
way. Take warm clothing with you: what starts as a warm,
sunny day can, and often does, change to mist and bitter
chill within minutes. Most visitors ride up in the shiny
new gondolas which recently replaced the old 27-seater
cable cars when the Table Mountain Aerial Cable Car

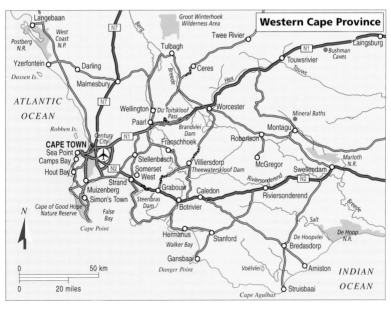

ROBBEN ISLAND

Just offshore to the west of of the suburb of Milnerton and visible from the summit of Table Mountain, lies Robben Island, where **Nelson Mandela** was incarcerated for much of his 27-year imprisonment. The island has served as a sheep farm, a penal settlement, a leper colony, a pauper camp, an infirmary and a lunatic asylum. The Island was recently proclaimed a World Heritage Site; trips take in the tiny cells (including Mandela's) and **Robert Sobukwe's** prison home. Half-day trips to the island can be booked through the Department of Tourism at the V&A Waterfront, tel: (021) 419-1300.

Company upgraded its facilities in 1997. The new cars, boasting revolving floors and a magnificent 360° view over the city, carry up to 65 individuals at a time. The six-minute trip may be taken at virtually any time of the year – from 08:00–22:00 December–April, 08:30–18:00 May–November. Because of the larger carrying capacity of the cars, queues are short and bookings are no longer taken.

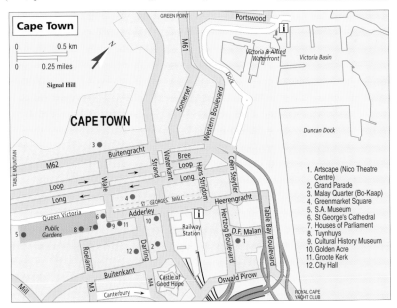

Cape Town

0   0.5 km

0   0.25 miles

1. Artscape (Nico Theatre Centre)
2. Grand Parade
3. Malay Quarter (Bo-Kaap)
4. Greenmarket Square
5. S.A. Museum
6. St George's Cathedral
7. Houses of Parliament
8. Tuynhuys
9. Cultural History Museum
10. Golden Acre
11. Groote Kerk
12. City Hall

Above: *The Heerengracht thoroughfare is part of the Foreshore, a flat expanse of land that was reclaimed from the sea.*

Central Cape Town ★

This is one of the few centres best explored on foot. A pleasant walk through the city centre should start in **Adderley Street**, the city's main thoroughfare. Making your way towards the mountain, the huge, glitzy **Golden Acre** and its underground and adjoining **Sun Gallery** complex of stores, specialty shops, cinemas and eating places is on the left, as is the flower market, where one can bargain for exquisite blooms with the good-humoured stall-holders; the Dutch Reformed **Groote Kerk**, noted for its fine woodwork; and the **Old Slave Lodge**, now part of the Cultural History Museum complex. At the top of Adderley Street is **St George's Cathedral**, which offers some fine stained-glass work, an angelic choir. Turn into **St George's Mall**, a nine-block, brick-paved pedestrian walkway lined with shops, arcades and umbrella-shaded bistros, enlivened by enthusiastic buskers. Pleasant digressions are cobblestoned **Greenmarket Square**, one of Africa's prettiest plazas and usually filled to capacity with market stalls, and **Long Street**. Once the vibrant centre of city life, this street is now rather seedy but it has a few good antique and book shops (Clarkes' reputation as an antiquarian book store and supplier of Africana works extends well beyond the city), two mosques, the elegant **Sendinggestig** (Missionary Society) church museum and some filigreed Victorian and Edwardian buildings.

The Public Gardens **

Formally known as **The Company's Garden** (it began life in the 1650s as Jan van Riebeeck's vegetable patch), this expanse of greenery lies beyond St George's Cathedral. It's a must for anyone interested in plants: more than 8000 different kinds of tree, shrub and flower – most of exotic origin – can be seen in the beautifully laid-out grounds. Running along the Gardens' eastern boundary is oak-lined **Government Avenue**, with benches for those who like to linger a while in the dappled shade. At the mountain end is an aviary and a shady tea garden (don't expect too much in the way of food and service).

Notable buildings around Government Avenue are the **Houses of Parliament** and Colonial Regency-style **Tuynhuys** (city office of the president); the **National Gallery**, which contains around 7000 works of art; the domed and twin-towered **Great Synagogue** and its neighbour, the **Old Synagogue**, housing treasures of the Jewish Museum; the **South African Museum**, whose Karoo fossils and Bushman exhibits are fascinating, and the adjacent **Planetarium**; and the **South African Library**, one of the world's first free libraries, which stages intriguing thematic exhibitions.

MUSEUMS AND GALLERIES

Koopmans-De Wet House on Strand Street in the city centre: yellowwood and stinkwood furniture, including 'riempie stools'.
Michaelis Collection (Old Town House), Greenmarket Square: 17th-century Dutch and Flemish paintings.
Natale Labia Museum, Muizenberg: fine furniture and works of art.
Rhodes Cottage, between Muizenberg and St James: Cecil Rhodes' last home.
Simon's Town Naval Museum: interesting naval and local history exhibits.

PICK OF THE WATERFRONT RESTAURANTS

• **Morton's on the Wharf**: New Orleans-inspired, Creole and spicy Cajun dishes from the Deep South
• **Ferryman's Tavern**: freshly brewed local beer and good pub food
• **The Sport's Café**: lively, abuzz with non-stop sport
• **Quay Four**: alfresco meals at the water's edge or à la carte dining upstairs
• **Panama Jack's**: old harbour, fantastic crayfish
• **Musselcracker**: Cape seafood buffet.

Left: *New cable cars take visitors up Table Mountain, itself part of the recently proclaimed Cape Peninsula National Park.*

Above: *Elegant charm is the keynote of the Victoria & Alfred Waterfront; part of its attraction is that visitors can observe boats at work in the busy harbour.*

Please note: there's a lot of poverty and unemployment in the city and surrounds, and muggings are a risk. Take the basic precautions. Strolling along well-used roads is safe in daylight hours, but safer in company.

The Waterfront ★★★

City and harbour has been reunited by the ambitious **Victoria & Alfred Waterfront** redevelopment scheme, a multibillion-dollar private venture that has borrowed ideas from San Francisco's harbour project, Boston's Quincy Market and others, but retains a lively character of its own. Among its various attractions are the **Two Oceans** – a world-class oceanarium complex housing both Atlantic and southern Indian Ocean species. Features include a functioning riverine ecosystem, a touch pool, and an 'underwater' tunnel – a walkway surpartially enclosed by glass. The larger-than-life screen and wraparound sound system of the sensational **Imax Cinema** make it a very popular drawcard. Restaurants, bistros and bars, speciality shops, craft markets, fish and produce markets, cinemas, hotels and a maritime museum are all under the roof of the Waterfront complex, and exciting new structures continue to be erected along the banks of the yacht basin and marina.

THEATRES

Theatres of note in and around Cape Town include:
• **Artscape (Nico Theatre centre)** on the Foreshore.
• **Baxter** theatre complex in Rosebank.
• **Theatre on the Bay** in Camps Bay
• **On Broadway** cabaret venue in Green Point.

This is a lived-in, workaday area as well as a fun place: fishing boats still use it (some as tourist craft); and office and residential complexes edge the border. It's highly recommended, though it does become crowded (and the service rushed) over weekends and holidays.

Bo-Kaap *

This inner suburb, on the lower slopes of **Signal Hill** west of the central area, is a splash of exotic culture in an otherwise standard city setting: a picturesque place of mosques and quaint flat-roofed 18th-century houses, and home to part of Cape Town's **Islamic** community, many of whom are descended from Indonesian slaves and political exiles brought in by the Dutch colonists. The name in translation means 'above Cape', though it is also known as the **Malay Quarter**. There is a small museum – a period house – *in situ* at 71 Wale Street. Don't wander around on your own, but rather take an organized tour (tel: (021) 26-1977).

Shopping

Cape Town's many craft markets are the place to shop for contemporary African art and artefacts, curios, ethnic jewellery, leatherware and clothing (although South Africa has a sophisticated clothing industry and boasts a number of top designers).

There are also plenty of antiques shops but beware of tourist traps; try **Long Street** and the **Church Street** open-air antique fair (open on Fridays). Open-air markets are held at **Greenmarket Square**, **St George's Mall**, the **Grand Parade** and the railway station, and offer fun shopping. You are likely to find a lot of junk, but, occasionally, a real bargain.

RHODES MEMORIAL

This tribute to 19th-century financier and visionary **Cecil Rhodes**, situated on the eastern slopes of Devil's Peak, was designed in grandly classical style as a 'temple' by the celebrated architect **Herbert Baker**. Kipling's farewell words to the 'immense and brooding spirit' are inscribed on a bust of Rhodes; G. F. Watts' statue, **'Physical Energy'**, is also part of the complex, which has a new restaurant attached.

Below: *The Victoria Wharf warehouse shelters a myriad specialty shops.*

Sunset Cruises

• **Teacher's Spirit of Adventure**: daily cruise with dinner, dancing and cabaret show; tel: (021) 419-3122.
• **Circe Launch**: sunset trip from Hout Bay to Cape Town harbour; sparkling wine and snacks; Oct to Apr; return bus trip available; tel: (021) 790-1040.
• **Sealink Tours**: cruise from Waterfront to Clifton; sparkling wine and souvenir champagne glass; Dec to Mar; tel: (021) 25-4480.

Northern Delights

The suburbs to the north and east of the central area, long neglected by the tourist, are now coming into their own with the development of major new venues. Notable among these is the **Century City** and its **Canal Walk** component, the southern hemisphere's largest and arguably most imaginative shopping centre. The complex has grown (and will continue to grow) rapidly to embrace restaurants, cinemas, science centre, hotel, convention centre, waterfront, small craft harbour, bird-rich wetlands and the lively **Ratanga Junction** theme park. The **Tyger Valley** mall, one of the country's biggest and best, is not too far away. Also on stream is the **GrandWest casino** and entertainment world at Goodwood, which includes gaming rooms, hotels, eateries, nightspots and an Olympic standard ice rink.

For sophisticated shoppers there's the **V&A Waterfront**, Claremont's stylish **Cavendish Square** and the grand new **Century City** and **Canal Walk** complex in Milnerton (*see* box left). Gold amd diamond jewellery are available tax free for overseas visitors.

Cape Peninsula

A leisurely day's drive around the Peninsula's coastline, a visit to the botanical gardens at Kirstenbosch, and wine tasting at Constantia's wine estates are some of the choice options available to the visitor to the Cape Peninsula.

To visit Cape Point, drive southwards along the coastal road from Sea Point to picturesque Llandudno, passing Bantry Bay, Clifton and Camps Bay (the imposing **Twelve Apostles**, an extension of the Table Mountain range, line the route on your left), and down to the fishing harbour of Hout Bay. Either continue inland through lovely Constantia and the scenic Ou Kaapse Weg ('Old Cape Road') or, if they've finished repairing the cliffside route, over spectacular Chapman's Peak Drive to

Kommetjie and Scarborough and on to the **Cape of Good Hope Nature Reserve** and **Cape Point**. An alternative route back to town would be along the east coast, past Boulders and Seaforth, through Simon's Town (steeped in naval history), Glencairn, Fish Hoek and Muizenberg, and on to Ladies Mile past Tokai and Constantia.

Cape Point ★★★

Often mistaken as the meeting place of the Atlantic and Indian oceans, Cape Point is Africa's second most southerly point after **Cape Agulhas**, the geographical meeting place of the two oceans. The headland is part of the extensive **Cape of Good Hope Nature Reserve** – itself part of the recently proclaimed **Cape Peninsula National Park** – a place of marvellous floral diversity (at its best in spring) and a sanctuary for grey rhebok, Cape mountain zebra, duiker, Cape fox, caracal, dassies and baboons. (do not feed or tease the baboons). Facilities include fishing and boating, picnic spots, a restaurant and a gift shop. There is also a selection of hiking paths (maps available at the entrance); of note is a short trail from Olifantsbos, skirting rock pools and leading to the wreck of the *Thomas T. Tucker*. A new funicular takes visitors up the hill to within walking distance of the Cape Point lighthouse.

> **HOUT BAY**
>
> This charming residential and fishing village on the Peninsula's west coast lies in a lovely valley bounded by wooded mountain slopes. Attractions include a pleasant beach and a picturesque harbour which houses the popular **Mariner's Wharf** (a fresh fish market and restaurants) and the **World of Birds,** one of southern Africa's largest bird parks (with landscaped walk-through aviaries). The small **Hout Bay Museum** organizes walks through the local countryside.

Opposite: *Llandudno Beach fringes the Peninsula's most delightful seaside village.*
Below: *Cape Point rises majestically above the southern ocean.*

Above: *One stretch of the Atlantic coastal road to Cape Point cuts through Chapman's Peak (closed for repairs in 2000), with its breathtaking views of the sea 600m (2000ft) below and, in the distance, the picturesque fishing harbour of Hout Bay.*

> **CAPE PENINSULA NATIONAL PARK**
>
> The entire Cape Peninsula, stretching from Signal Hill to Cape Point and including Table Mountain, was declared a national park in May 1998. The new Cape Peninsula National Park covers approximately 30,000ha (74,000 acres) of both state and private land, and includes within its protected boundaries thousands of animal and plant species – including the *fynbos* of the unique Cape Floral Kingdom – making it eligible for status as a World Heritage Site.

Kirstenbosch National Botanical Gardens ★★★

On the eastern slopes of the Table Mountain range, above the affluent southern suburbs, lies Kirstenbosch, one of the world's most celebrated botanic gardens. An astonishing array of flowering plants (around one quarter of southern Africa's 24,000 species) are cultivated here: proteas, pelargoniums, ericas, mesembryanthemums, ferns, cycads of ancient origin and much else. There are delightful walks through herb and fragrance gardens, a pelargonium koppie, a cycad amphitheatre; trails lead through the forests of stinkwood, yellowwood and silver trees; the birdlife – particularly the sugarbirds, drawn to the vast protaceae in the Garden – is enchanting. An impressive new Visitors' Centre and gift shop is located near the entrance. A Garden Shop at the entrance sells plants, gifts and books, and the restaurant is a popular venue for light Sunday lunches and teas, and during the summer months, for outdoor champagne breakfasts (bring your own bubbly). Summer concerts are held on Sunday evenings, and a wonderful way to spend the afternoon is to take a stroll through the Garden followed by a lazy picnic before the concert begins. Check the newspapers for up-to-date details.

Constantia Wine Estates ★★★

There are currently three estates in the beautiful Constantia valley, and together they form the local 'wine route'. **Groot Constantia**, the oldest and stateliest of the homesteads, dates from the late 17th century and is notable for its architecture, period furniture, two-storeyed wine cellar, museum and lovely grounds (the oak-lined avenue leads to an ornamental pool). For visitors there are daily wine sales, with some superlative vintages on offer, cellar tours, a horse and carriage for hire, picnic lunches on the pretty, shaded lawns and three restaurants.

Klein Constantia is smaller and more private, and the **Buitenverwachting** homestead houses one of the country's best restaurants. Ticket prices to the summer concerts (jazz and classical music) on Buitenverwachting's sprawling lawn, girded by giant oaks and vineyards, include a bottle of the estate's excellent wine. Bring a picnic basket and a blanket. Check the newspaper for concert details. Visit the nearby **Old Cape Farm Stall** for high-quality South African fruits, preserves and a tantalizing range of gourmet delicacies.

THE WINELANDS

The winelands of the Cape comprise a region of grand mountain ranges, fertile valleys, vineyards and orchards heavy with fruit, and of homesteads built in the distinctive and gracious style known as **Cape Dutch**. These were the first rural areas to be taken over by the early

Below: The historic homestead of Klein Constantia, on the Cape Peninsula's only wine route.

Above: *Boschendal, one of the winelands' beautiful and historic estates. The homestead is a fine example of the Cape Dutch style and dates from 1812.*

POINTS OF INTEREST IN AND
AROUND STELLENBOSCH

** Oom Samie se Winkel: charming general dealer from a bygone era.
** Oude Libertas Centre: stunning setting for open-air music, opera and drama (picnicking permitted on shaded lawns). Check newspaper for details.
* Van Ryn Brandy Cellar: musical events; guided tours (weekdays only) offer some insight into brandy-making.
* Bergkelder: the cellars have been carved out of the hillside.
* Libertas Parva: houses the fascinating Stellenryck Wine Museum.

white colonists: they began infiltrating the traditional lands of the Khoisan people of the interior in the 1660s, turning the countryside over to pasture, the growing of wheat and, increasingly, the cultivation of wine grapes. The farms prospered, the colony expanded, and a number of small towns were founded: **Stellenbosch** in 1679, **Franschhoek** ('French corner', named for its Huguenot settlers) 10 years later, to be followed by **Paarl**, **Wellington**, **Tulbagh**, **Worcester**, **Robertson** and others, all of them worth visiting for their history and the beauty of their surrounds.

Stellenbosch ***

Stellenbosch is less than an hour's drive from Cape Town, and lies in the Eerste River Valley beneath the Papegaaiberg. Founded in the late 17th century, the town is one built on history – a fact that is evident in its original watering system, old churchyards and gabled buildings, many of which can be seen along the oak-lined streets such as **Dorp Street**, around **Die Braak** (the village green) and in the **Village Museum** complex. Stellenbosch is a leading centre of learning; university and town are harmoniously integrated. It is also the starting point of a major wine route: 22 estates and cellars are within a 12km (7 miles) radius.

Paarl *

The biggest of the wineland towns, Paarl was founded in 1720 and named after the granite rock that resembles a giant pearl on the overlooking mountain. The mountain and its surrounds are maintained as an attractive nature reserve; there's a circular route to the top; well worth a short detour is the **Mill Stream wildflower garden**.

Paarl's long main street is shaded by oaks and jacarandas; among features of interest in and around the area are the **KWV** complex – the world's largest wine co-operative – and its historic **Laborie** homestead; the **Wagonmakers museum**; the **Oude Pastorie**, which houses some fine old Cape furniture; and the **Taal-monument**, or Afrikaans Language Monument.

Not far out of Paarl is **Nederburg**, an elegant Cape Dutch homestead and probably South Africa's best-known wine-making estate. It is set in a wide sweep of countryside mantled by vines. The Nederburg wine auction, held around April each year, is a huge social business occasion (by invitation only).

Franschhoek **

This small centre was founded in 1688 on land granted to **Huguenot** refugees. Little remains of the original French

> **FRANSCHHOEK'S FORTÉ: FIRST-CLASS DINING**
>
> ● **Le Quartier Français**, Huguenot Road: award-winner, exquisite French-influenced, Cape-style cuisine, tel: (021) 876-2151.
> ● **La Petite Ferme**, Pass Road: sweeping views of the valley, great food, tel: (021) 876-3016.
> ● **La Maison de Chamonix**, Uitkyk Road: voted among the country's top three popular restaurants, tel: (021) 876-2393.
> ● **Chez Michel**, Huguenot Road: French bistro atmosphere, tel: (021) 876-2671.
> ● **Polfyntjies**, fresh country cooking, tel: (021) 876-3217.

Below: *The Huguenot Memorial honours the contribution made by the early French immigrants.*

SELECT WINE ESTATES

★★★ Boschendal: 17th-century Cape Dutch manor offering a buffet of traditional Cape fare and superb grounds ideal for picnics.
★★★ Spier: take the Spier Express to the recently upgraded estate, with its wildlife and music attractions.
★★★ Fairview: makes a variety of cheeses from estate's own livestock's milk; peacocks roam the gardens.
★★ Backsberg: tasting under the oaks in summer; self-guided cellar tours; small wine museum.
★★ Delheim: described as a 'tourist's jewel and photographer's paradise'.
★★ Blaauwklippen: charming, gabled house; museum; coach rides.

Above: *A vegetable and fruit stall near Robertson; the surrounding country-side boasts a dozen or so thoroughbred stud farms.*

culture except the names of the surrounding estates. The most notable features of Franschhoek are the first-class restaurants nestled in its vine-covered valley. The graceful **Huguenot Memorial** and its next-door museum complex stand at the end of the town's long main street.

The Wine Routes

Touring the various wine routes in and around Constantia, Stellenbosch, Franschhoek, Paarl, Worcester and Robertson is a very pleasant way to spend one's day. There are hundreds of wineries and estates, so visitors with limited time will be able to cover only a fraction of them. A visit to four or maybe five is the most you can expect to manage in a day's outing.

Most cellars offer tours (at set times) and tastings, and there's no limit to the number of wines you're allowed to try, though many of the places charge a small initial fee. Some run excellent restaurants; at others there are farm stalls selling local specialities, gift shops, and sometimes galleries or museums.

SCENIC DAY DRIVES
Four Passes Fruit Route ★★

If you're in a motoring mood, the scenically splendid Four Passes drive leads you from Cape Town to Stellenbosch, and over the **Helshoogte Pass** which towers above the Drakenstein valley area. It then takes you past Boschendal Estate and Franschhoek (*see* p. 115), over the rugged **Franschhoek Pass** and through the apple orchards of Elgin and Grabouw, before bringing you home over the Hottentots–Holland range via **Sir Lowry's Pass** and through Somerset West. You may also like to take **Viljoen's Pass** to Vyeboom and Villiersdorp.

If you feel inclined to taste a few wines, pay a visit to Anglo-American's new multimillion-rand wine cellar on the **Vergelegen Estate**. Designed by a Parisian architect, the winery is built into the hillside and offers a 360-degree view unequalled by any Cape wine farm. You can enjoy a light lunch or stay for tea; visits to the winery are by appointment. Nature lovers shouldn't miss a visit to the nearby **Helderberg Nature Reserve**, which offers lovely scenery, as well as interesting flora and birdlife.

CAPE AGULHAS

Proximately 100km (62 miles) to the east of Cape Town is Cape Agulhas, the southern-most point of the African continent. The name is derived from the Portuguese word for 'needles' (the early navigators found that their compasses weren't affected here by magnetic deviation). Completed in 1848, the **Cape Agulhas lighthouse** is the second oldest in South Africa, and has been declared a national monument. A lighthouse museum (the only one of its kind in the country) offers a range of fascinating displays that trace lighthouse development from ancient times to the present.

Certainly worth an hour or two of one's time is the **shipwreck museum** in nearby **Bredasdorp**.

Above Left: *The scenic Helderberg Nature Reserve: rich in flora and wildlife.*
Opposite: *The Old Harbour at Hermanus has been preserved as a museum, and as a memorial dedicated to the hardy fisher- men of yesteryear.*

Above: *Alfresco enjoyment at Melkbosskerm, one of the West Coast's marvellously informal outdoor seafood restaurants. The region is renowned for its crayfish.*
Opposite: *The springtime glory of Namaqualand.*

Hermanus ★★★

From Cape Town, make your way through Somerset West along the main N2 highway which leads over the mountains, beyond which are the plentiful fruit orchards of Elgin and Grabouw, and then on to the pretty cliffside town of Hermanus.

Best known for its **southern right whales,** Hermanus has become quite a tourist attraction during the midwinter months when these ponderous but oddly graceful mammals make their way into the bay to calve, their arrival heralded by the town's official '**whale crier**'. Excellent lunches are served by Hermanus's **Marine Hotel**, a place still run in the grand Victorian tradition.

A more scenic drive, and only slightly longer, takes you along the coast from Gordon's Bay past Betty's Bay; the **Harold Porter Nature Reserve** here is worth a visit.

West Coast ★★

A pleasant excursion is that leading up the west coast to **Langebaan Lagoon**, one of the country's finest wetlands and a bird-watcher's paradise.

Visit the **West Coast National Park** (headquarters at Langebaan Lodge), Langebaan village (boat trips, country club, Club Mykonos – a Greek-style entertainment and time-share complex) and, on the northern side of the lagoon, the tiny village of Paternoster, a popular crayfishing spot, is not far away from **Saldanha Bay** (mussels, crayfishing and boat trips).

NAMAQUALAND – FLOWERING DESERT

At first sight the plains of Namaqualand, the arid western coastal strip that stretches up to the Gariep River and Namibia in the north, seems too harsh and inhospitable to support any but the hardiest, least appealing kinds of life. Yet the region is unbelievably rich in succulents and flowering annuals. After the winter rains – between **late July** and **September** – the land is briefly and gloriously mantled by great carpets of wildflowers.

Namaqualand is home to about 4000 different floral species, most of which belong to the daisy and mesembryanthemum (known locally as *vygies*) groups but there are also aloes and lilies, perennial herbs and a host of others. The small, low-growing plants are drought resistant, the seeds lying dormant during the long dry months. Then, after the winter rains but before the onset of the burning desert winds – when they sense the impending arrival of the pollinators – they burst into bright life, maturing in a matter of days to magically transform the countryside.

It's worth making the long journey to witness the spectacle. Organized tours are available; **Specialised Tours**, for instance, offer a day trip that embraces Langebaan Lagoon, Mamre and Darling; en route you're treated to a seafood lunch and, of course, to marvellous wildflower displays. For those who have the time, a longer three-day tour is recommended.

WHEN AND WHERE TO SEE FLOWERS

The best months are normally **Aug** to **Sep**, but as this varies from year to year, call Flowerline first, tel: (021) 418-3705 at the Western Cape Tourism Board.
● The most spectacular displays are normally in the **Postberg Nature Reserve**, around **Clanwilliam** and the **Biedouw Valley, Van-rhynsdorp, Nieuwoudt-ville, Kamieskroon** and **Springbok**.
● On sunny days flowers open between 10:00 and 16:30; on overcast days they do not open at all.
● A flower tour can be accomplished in one day (for example, if you visit Postberg, near Langebaan), but allow two to three days for the major routes.
● If you set aside several days to view the flowers, choose private accommodation for a more personal touch, as the hotels are generally rather average.
● Take warm clothing, as mornings and evenings can still be very chilly.

Western Cape Province at a Glance

Sept and **Oct** (spring): pleasant for the crisp air and fynbos in flower; **March** and **April:** (autumn) for balmy, still days that have lost their scorch.

Cape Town's **international airport** 22km (14 miles) outside the city. Shuttle bus service links airport with Cape Town railway station (buses depart from main vehicle entrance, outside plat-form 24). To book contact Cape Town Tourism.

Eastern peninsula and northern areas served by **rail network**; timetables available from Cape Town Tourism. Waterfront linked to city centre by **shuttle bus**; leaves from outside Information Bureau, Adderley St. Blue-and-yellow **Rikki**, inexpensive cabs, cater for small groups who like to devise their own tours, tel: (021) 23-4888. **Car-hire** firms represented at airport and city centre.

Cape Town
Mount Nelson, Gardens, tel: (021) 23-1000, fax: 24-7472. One of the country's oldest and most elegant.
Victoria & Alfred Waterfront Hotel, Pierhead, tel: (021) 419-6677, fax: 419-8955. Superb views of Table Bay.
The Bay, Camps Bay seafront, tel: (021) 438-4444, fax: 438-4455. Pristinely modern.

Cape Sun, central city, tel: (021) 23-1861.
Cellars–Hohenhort Country House Hotel, Constantia, tel: (021) 794-2137. Originally an 18th-century wine cellar.
Vineyard Hotel, Newlands, tel: (021) 683-3044, fax: 683-3365. Historic hotel (1799), beautiful gardens.

BUDGET ACCOMMODATION
Breakwater Lodge, Waterfront, tel: (021) 406-1911, fax: 406-1070. Good value.
City Lodge, Mowbray, tel: (021) 685-7944, fax: 685-7997; V&A Waterfront, tel: (021) 419-9450, fax: 419-0460.
Holiday Inn Garden Courts: De Waal, Greenmarket Square, St George's Mall, Newlands, call Southern Sun Group toll free 0800-11-7711.

Stellenbosch
D'Ouwe Werf, 30 Church Street, tel: (021) 887-1608, fax: 887-4626. Small, historic. The **Lanzerac**, Lanzerac Road, tel: (021) 887-1132, fax: 887-2310. Gracious historic estate.
L'Auberge Rozendal, Omega Rd, Jonkershoek, tel: (021) 883-8737. On working wine farm.

Paarl
Grande Roche, Plantasie St, tel: (021) 863-2727, fax: 863-2220. Set among vineyards; offers international standards.
Mountain Shadows, off Klein Drakenstein Road, tel: (021) 862-3192, fax: 862-6796. Inviting country house.

Roggeland Country House, Noorder-Paarl, tel: (021) 868-2501, fax: 868-2113. Charming, superb cuisine

Franschhoek
L'Auberge du Quartier Française, cnr Berg and Wilhelmina sts, tel: (021) 876-2151, fax: 876-3105. Maintains superb international quality.
Le Ballon Rouge, Reservoir St East, tel: (021) 876-2651. Restored Victorian guest house, seven rooms.

Somerset West
Lord Charles Hotel, corner Stellenbosch and Faure roads, tel: (021) 855-1040, fax: 855-1107. Luxurious.

Cape Town
Blues, Camps Bay, tel: (021) 438-2040. California-style, overlooks palm-fringed shore.
Buitenverwachting, Constantia, tel: (021) 794-3522. One of the very best; innovative cuisine
Constantia Uitsig, Uitsig Farm, tel: (021) 794-6500. Set among wine estates.
The Green Dolphin, V&A Waterfront, tel: (021) 423-1651. Seafood and live jazz.
Floris Smit Huijs, city centre, tel: (021) 423-3414. Stylish, very fine food.
Jacksons, Peninsula hotel, tel: (021) 439-8302. Imaginative dishes from around the world.
Mamma Africa, Long Street, tel: (021) 424-8634. African continental food, lively bar.

Western Cape Province at a Glance

Bayfront Blu, Two Oceans Aquarium, V&A Waterfront, tel: (021) 419-9068. Seafood and African dishes, views.

Ethnic restaurants

Africa Café, Observatory, tel: (021) 447-9553. Dishes from Cameroon, Kenya, Zambia and Mozambique.

Cape Malay Kitchen, Cellars-Hohenort Hotel, Constantia, tel: (021) 794-2137. Cape Malay food, alcohol permitted.

Kaapse Tafel, Gardens, tel: (021) 423-1651. Reliably good, traditional Cape cuisine.

Stellenbosch

De Kelder, tel: (021) 883-3797. Built in 1790, traditional Cape dishes.

Lanzerac Hotel restaurant, tel: (021) 887-1132. Cosmopolitan cuisine.

Doornbosch, tel: (021) 887-5079. revamped, specializes in superb Italian fare.

Lord Neethling, tel: (021) 886-6163. Historical monument. Oriental dishes,

Paarl

Bosman's, Grande Roche Hotel, tel: (021) 863-2727. Best in the country.

Rhebokskloof, tel: (021) 863-8606. Wine estate with three restaurants, and a small lake.

Troubadour, Rozenfontein, tel: (021) 863-3556. Swiss cuisine, Victorian house.

Franschhoek

See page 115.

Somerset West

Garden Terrace, Lord Charles Hotel, tel: (021) 855-1040. Cape Malay dishes, also buffet.

L'Auberge du Paysan, tel: (021) 842-2008. top award-winner for French cuisine.

See page 115.

TOURS AND EXCURSIONS

Balloon tours (plus champagne), tel: (021) 863-3192. Wineland Ballooning.

Canoeing in the winelands: Felix Unite River Adventures, tel: (021) 683-6433; River Rafters, tel: (021) 712-5094.

Coach tours: Peninsula, Winelands, West Coast Garden Route, Hylton Ross, Mother City Tours, and many others; contact Cape Town Tourism.

Helicopter trips over Peninsula or Winelands: Civair, tel: (021) 419-5182, Court Helicopters, tel: (021) 934-0560.

Train trips: contact the Spier Wine Estate for a train trip to the recently revamped estate and its wildlife attractions, tel: (021) 881-3096.

Cape Town arts and culture website: www.gocapetown.co.za

USEFUL CONTACTS

Cape Town International Airport, tel: (021) 937-1200.

Cape Town Tourism, Visitor's Centre, Burg Street, tel: (021) 426-4260. Information and help on your visit.

Computicket, theatre/cinema bookings, tel: (021) 918-8910.

Garden Route Tourism, tel: (044) 873-6314, fax: 884-0688.

Hermanus Publicity Association, tel: (0283) 22629.

MTN Whale Hotline, tel: 800 910 1028.

MTN Flowerline, tel: 800 910 1028 or Cape Town Tourism, (021) 426-4267.

Robben Island: for official tours, tel: (021) 419-1300.

Stellenbosch Publicity Association, tel: (021) 883-3584/9633, fax: 883-8017.

Table Mountain Cableway, tel: (021) 424-8181; website: www.tablemountain.co.za

V&A Waterfront Visitors' Centre, tel: (021) 418-2369.

Winelands Regional Tourism, tel: (021) 872-0686, fax: 872-0534.

West Coast Tourism, tel: (022) 433-2380, fax: 433-22127.

CAPE TOWN	J	F	M	A	M	J	J	A	S	O	N	D
AVERAGE TEMP. °C	21	21	20	17	15	13	12	13	14	16	18	20
AVERAGE TEMP. °F	70	70	68	63	59	55	54	55	57	61	64	68
HOURS OF SUN DAILY	11	11	10	8	6	6	6	7	8	9	10	11
SEA TEMP. °C	15	14	13	13	12	12	12	13	13	14	14	14
SEA TEMP. °F	59	57	55	55	54	54	54	55	55	57	57	57
RAINFALL mm	12	18	22	56	77	98	97	74	42	33	14	14
RAINFALL ins.	0.5	0.5	1	2	3	4	4	3	2	1.5	0.5	0.5
DAYS OF RAINFALL	7	6	7	9	14	14	14	15	13	11	8	8

Travel Tips

Tourist Information

Satour (the South African Tourism Board) maintains offices in, among other countries, the United Kingdom (London), the United States (New York and Los Angeles), France (Paris), Germany (Frankfurt), Israel (Tel Aviv), Italy (Milan), Japan (Tokyo), the Netherlands, Belgium and Scandinavia (principal office Amsterdam), Switzerland and Austria (principal office Zürich), Taiwan (Taipei), and Zimbabwe (Harare).

Satour's headquarters are at 442 Riegel Avenue South, Erasmusrand, Pretoria; Private Bag X164, Pretoria 0001; tel: (012) 347-0600. Satour operates regional offices in major centres. The country is well represented on the Internet; quickest and most efficient way to find out more about South African destinations and other tourism information is via the **Ananzi South Africa** search engine, website: www.ananzi.co.za

Major centres and tourist areas have **publicity associations** which provide up-to-date information, free of charge, on everything from recreation to transport and accommodation. Contact addresses and numbers for many of these appear in the relevant chapters of this book. **Computicket**, which has branches countrywide, handles most concert, theatre and cinema bookings. For contact details, consult the relevant directory for a specific region.

Entry Documents

All visitors need a valid passport for entry into South Africa. Most foreign nationals, how-ever, are exempt from visa requirements, including citizens of the United States, Canada and the European Community, as well as the following countries: Australia, New Zealand, Japan, Namibia, Austria, Brazil, Chile, Botswana, Ireland, Singapore and Switzerland.

Health Requirements

Visitors from or passing through a yellow fever zone (most of tropical Africa and South America) must be able to produce a valid International Certificate of Vaccination. Air travellers who only pass through the airports of such a zone are exempt from the requirement. Note that cholera and smallpox certificates are no longer needed, and no Aids screening procedure is in force.

Air Travel

The country's major points of entry are Johannesburg (which also serves Pretoria) and Cape Town's international airports. Durban's airport also has international status. **Domestic services:** Among domestic centres served by South African Airways are Bloemfontein, Cape Town, Durban, East London, George, Johannesburg, Kimberley, Port Elizabeth, Pretoria, Pietersburg, Nelspruit, Mmabatho and Upington. Small airlines serve the lesser towns and main tourist destinations. Air charter services (including helicopter hire) are widely available.

Road Travel

South Africa has an extensive and well-signposted road

network comprising some 200,000km (124,280 miles) of national and provincial highways. Surfaces are generally in very good condition, though the going can be a bit rugged in the remoter and hillier country areas.

Driver's licence: You must carry this with you at all times. Zimbabwe, Mozambique, Namibia, Botswana, Lesotho and Swaziland licences are valid in South Africa. So too are other foreign licences, provided they carry a photograph and are either printed in English or accompanied by an English-language certificate of authenticity.

Alternatively, obtain an International Driving Permit before your departure.

Road rules and signs: In South Africa, one drives on the left. The general speed limit on national highways, urban freeways and other major routes is 120 kph (75 mph); that on secondary (rural) roads is 100 kph (60 mph), and in built-up areas 60 kph (35 mph) unless otherwise indicated.

Main roads are identified by colour and number rather than by name. Using a good map (one which incorporates the route marker system), the visitor should have little difficulty in finding his/her way around city and country.

Car hire: Avis, Imperial (incorporating Hertz), Budget and other, smaller, rental firms are well represented in the major centres. Airports and some of the bigger game parks have car-hire facilities.

ROAD SIGNS IN AFRIKAANS

Words to watch out for are:
Links (left)
Regs (right)
Stad (city)
Lughawe (airport)
Straat (street)
Weg (road)
Rylaan (avenue)
Hou (keep)
Slegs (only)
Oop (open)
Gesluit (closed)
Gevaar (beware hazard)
Verbode (forbidden)
Ompad (detour)
Tuin ('garden' but often used in conjunction with 'wild' – e.g. **wildtuin** – to denote a park or reserve)
Strand (beach)
Hawe (harbour).
Note that in South Africa a 'robot' is a set of traffic lights.

Insurance: Your motor vehicle must be covered by a Third Party Insurance policy; if you're hiring a car, the rental firm will make the appropriate arrangements; for overland visitors, insurance tokens are available at Beitbridge and other major border control posts.

Maps: Excellent regional and city maps are available from Satour, the Automobile Association, from major book stores and airport kiosks. Recommended are those in the *Globetrotter* series.

Petrol: Cities, towns and main routes are very well served by filling stations. Many of these stay open 24 hours a day, others from 06:00 to 18:00. Petrol, either Super or Premium, is sold in litres. Note that on the Highveld, because of its altitude, the petrol has a lower octane rating (Super is 93, Premium 87; while on the coast, Super is 97 and Premium 93). Rather use the Super or Premium rating as a guide. Pump attendants see to your fuel and other needs.

Automobile Association: The AA is the country's biggest motoring club, and provides a wide range of services, including assistance with breakdowns and other emergencies, accommodation reservations and advice on touring, caravanning, camping, places of interest, insurance and car hire. Maps and brochures are available. These services are offered to visitors who belong to the AA or any affiliated motoring organization. The AA's headquarters are in AA House, 66 Korte Street, Braamfontein (Johannesburg) 2001; tel: (011) 799-1000. For AA offices in other centres, consult the relevant telephone directory.

Coach travel: Luxury coach services link the major centres (Greyhound, Intercape Ferreira, Translux, Trancity); tour operators spread the network wider, taking in game parks, scenic attractions and other tourist venues. For details, consult your travel agent or the local publicity association.

What to Pack

South Africa enjoys long hot summers and generally mild winters; people dress informally, though 'smart casual' wear is often required after dark at theatres and other art/entertainment venues, and by the more sophisticated hotels and restaurants. Beach wear is acceptable only on the beach; casual clothing is customary at holiday resorts and in the game areas.

For the summer months (October to April), pack lightweight garments and a hat but include a jacket or jersey for the cooler, and occasionally chilly, nights. Most of the country is in the summer-rainfall zone, so bring an umbrella or raincoat. For the winter months, be sure to pack warm clothing.

Money Matters

The South African currency unit is the Rand, divided into 100 cents. Coins are issued in denominations of 1c, 5c, 10c, 20c, 50c, R1, R2 and R5; notes in denominations of R5, R10, R20, R50, and recently, R100 and R200. Coinage designs were also recently changed, and some denominations circulate in two forms; beware the superficial similarity between some of the smaller and larger denominations.

Currency exchange: Foreign currency can be converted into rands at banks, Bureaux de Change and through such authorized dealers as Thomas Cook and American Express.

Banks: Normal banking hours in major centres are 09:00 to 15:30 on weekdays and 08:30 or 09:00 to 11:00 on Saturdays. There are currency exchange and banking facilities at the three international

airports. Traveller's cheques can be cashed at any banking institution and at many hotels and shops.

Credit cards: Most hotels, restaurants, shops, car-hire companies and tour operators accept international credit cards (American Express, Bank of America, Visa, Diners' Club, MasterCard). Note that you cannot buy petrol with a credit card.

Value Added Tax: VAT, currently at 14 per cent, is levied on most goods (basic foodstuffs are exempt); foreign visitors can claim back the tax paid on goods to be taken out of the country and whose total value exceeds R250. For this you'll need to present (at the point of exit) your passport, the goods themselves and the relevant invoices.

Tipping: Provided the service is satisfactory, it's usual to tip porters, waiters/waitresses, taxi drivers, room attendants and golf caddies. Tipping petrol attendants is optional, though a window-wash and a cheerful smile merit recognition. Gratuities for quantifiable services (waiters, taxi drivers) should amount to at least 10 per cent of the cost of the service; for nonquantifiable services of a minor nature (porterage, for example) it's customary to offer a tip of plus-minus R5.

Service charges: Hotels may not by law levy a charge for general services (though there's often a telephone service loading, sometimes a hefty one). Restaurants may levy such a charge; few do so.

Accommodation

A voluntary grading system, covering all types of accommodation, was recently introduced; ratings range from one to five stars.

The best South African hotels are of international standard but, generally speaking, local hoteliers still have a lot to learn from their counterparts in Europe, North America and the Pacific Rim. Major groups are **Sun International** (casino hotels), **Southern Sun/Holiday Inns**, **Karos**, **Protea**, **City Lodge** and others. Most of them fall into the middle price range, but Protea establishments tend to retain a more individual character, and offer quality and good value.

Rather than restricting visitors' options to the major hotel chains, it is recommended that they choose some of the country getaways and guest farms. There is a great variety of guest houses often close to the major tourist areas (Mpumalanga, Northern KwaZulu-Natal, the Garden Route, the Cape Peninsula, Winelands and West Coast). You're assured of good food and personal service.

The larger South African game parks and reserves (run by the **South African National Parks**, tel: (012) 343-1991, and those in KwaZulu-Natal by the **KwaZulu-Natal Nature Conservation Service**, tel: (033) 845-1000), offer comfortable, mainly self-catering accommodation in fully-equipped chalets, bungalows, cottages and less sophisticated huts, though many of the rest camps in the parks and reserves also boast an à la carte restaurant.

It is worth noting that these two controlling bodies play a very important role in the conservation of the country's national parks, while aiming for a sensitive balance between ecology and material benefit to neighbouring impoverished communities.

Game lodges are an increasingly prominent feature in the South African hospitality business. Usually located in private game reserves and on game farms, these cater largely for fairly affluent people who like to live well while they explore the ways of the wild; most lodges pride themselves on the degree of personal attention lavished on each guest, and on the skill of their rangers and trackers.

Self-catering options are varied and numerous, ranging from the rudimentary hiking hut through holiday apartments and cottages to the well-appointed, even luxurious, resort chalet.

Bed-and-breakfast accommodation is becoming increasingly popular, and many residents in the major tourist areas are making their homes available to visitors; for those who enjoy a warmer and more personal touch, this type of accommodation is ideal.

For detailed information, consult a travel agent, Satour or the relevant regional publicity association.

Trading Hours

At the time of writing these were subject to review and change; Sunday trading hours, in particular, are likely to become a lot less restrictive. Normal shopping and business hours are 08:30 to 17:00 Mondays to Fridays and 08:30 to 13:00 on Saturdays. However, many of the larger supermarkets and the more enterprising shopping complexes close later on weekdays and stay open on Saturday afternoons, Sunday mornings and over some of the public holidays.

Bars usually open at 10:00 and close at 23:00 on weekdays and Saturdays; nightclubs and some city bars remain open until 02:00 or later on weekdays.

Public Holidays

1 January (New Year's Day)
March/April (Good Friday, Easter Monday)
27 April (Freedom Day)
1 May (Workers' Day)
16 June (Youth Day)
9 August (Women's Day)
24 September (Heritage Day)
16 December (Day of Reconciliation)
25 December (Christmas Day)
26 December (Day of Good Will)
The Jewish, Islamic and Hindu communities observe special holy days.

Measurements

South Africa uses the metric system. A conversion chart appears below.

Telephones

The telecommunications system is almost fully automatic; one can dial direct to most centres in South (and southern) Africa and to most parts of the world. Telephone directories list the dialling codes; facsimile transmission (fax) facilities are widely available.
Enquiries: Should you find that a number you need is not listed in the telephone directory, or the number has changed, dial 1023.

Time

Throughout the year, South African Standard Time is two hours ahead of Greenwich Mean (or Universal Standard) Time, one hour ahead of

CONVERSION CHART		
FROM	**TO**	**MULTIPLY BY**
Millimetres	inches	0·0394
Metres	yards	1·0936
Metres	feet	3·281
Kilometres	miles	0·6214
Kilometres square	Square miles	0.386
Hectares	acres	2·471
Litres	pints	1·760
Kilograms	pounds	2·205
Tonnes	tons	0·984
To convert Celsius to Fahrenheit:	x 9 ÷ 5 + 32	

Central European Winter Time, and seven hours ahead of the USA's Eastern Standard Winter Time.

Electricity

Generally, urban power systems are 220/230 volts AC at 50 cycles a second; Pretoria's system generates 250 volts; Port Elizabeth's 220/250 volts. Plugs are 5-amp 2-pin or 15-amp 3-pin (round pins). Not all electric shavers will fit hotel and game-park plug points; visitors should seek advice about adaptors from a local electrical supplier.

Water

South African tap water is extremely palatable and perfectly safe to drink.

Medical Services

Visitors are responsible for their own medical arrangements, and are urged to take out medical insurance before departure. Private doctors are listed in the telephone directory under **'Medical Practitioners'**. Hospital admissions are usually arranged through a private practitioner, but in an emergency a visitor may telephone or go directly to the casualty department of a General Hospital or, in the smaller centres, to any public medical facility. Hospitals are listed under 'H' in the telephone directory.

Health Hazards

Malaria: The disease is prevalent in the Northern Province, Mpumalanga, and Northern KwaZulu-Natal. If you're plan-

ning to visit one of these areas, embark on a course of anti-malaria tablets before starting out. Tablets are available from local pharmacies, however some are only available on prescription, so make sure that you visit a pharmacist well in advance of your trip. Many prophylactics have to be taken a week before visiting an infested area, and medication continues for up to six weeks after. Note that some strains of this disease are becoming immune to chloroquine (one of the most common anti-malarial drugs) so rather use a substitute prophylactic.

Bilharzia: Also known as schistosomiasis, this debilitating waterborne disease is caused by a parasitical worm common in the lower-lying northern and eastern regions. Be circumspect about swimming in rivers and dams unless the assurances are clear that they are bilharzia free.

Aids: Although the incidence of full-blown Aids in South Africa remained low during the early 1990s, the disease is now reaching critical proportions. The risk of contracting Aids, however, is no greater here than in any other country, provided that the standard and well-publicized precautions are taken.

Creepy crawlies: South Africa has its fair share of snakes, spiders, scorpions and sundry stinging insects, but surprisingly few travellers, even those on safari, suffer serious attack or even discomfort. However, those

who are spending a holiday in the bush, or on walking trails, should obviously be more wary, and follow the advice of their ranger or group leader. For protection against ticks (the small red, hard-backed one can transmit tick-bite fever), wear long trousers on walks through long grass and apply insect repellant to bare legs and arms.

Emergencies

The national number for an ambulance is 10177 and for police emergency 10111, while the emergency number from a mobile or cellphone is 112. These numbers should, however, only be used if the caller believes life, limb or property is threatened.

Among personal crisis help services are **Lifeline** and **Alcoholics Anonymous**; both are listed in the regional telephone directories.

Security

The transition to a fully democratic order in South Africa has in many ways proved traumatic; there is a great deal of poverty around, and the crime rate in some areas is high. Take the same precautions as you would, say, in central New York; don't walk alone at night in either city or suburb; avoid deserted and poorer areas, unless you're with a conducted group; don't carry large sums of cash around with you; don't leave valuables in your room (use the hotel's safety deposit box).

INDEX